THE SAINT'S COMMUNION WITH GOD

by William Strong
with chapters by C. Matthew McMahon

COPYRIGHT INFORMATION

TABLE OF CONTENTS

MEET WILLIAM STRONG
By C. Matthew McMahon, Ph.D., Th.D.

William Strong, A.M. (d. 1654) was a faithful minister of the Gospel of Jesus Christ who received his education in Katherine-hall, Cambridge. Here he was chosen as fellow of the college. (The master of the college was the famous Dr. Richard Sibbes.) On leaving the university Strong was presented with being minister in Long Crichill in Dorsetshire, where he continued until he was forced to flee from the cavaliers. He then fled to London, where he often preached before parliament, was chosen one of the additional divines to the Westminster Assembly, and minister of St. Dunstan's in the West. After some time he gathered a congregation following the church government of the *Independents*, which assembled in Westminster Abbey, and was composed of many parliament men and important people residing in Westminster. He was chosen to the office of *pastor* here on December 9, 1650, on which occasion he delivered a sermon on the, *order of a gospel church.* He was afterwards nominated one of the triers for the approbation of preachers.[1]

---

[1] *cf.* Wood's *Athens, Oxod.* vol. ii. p. 139; Edmund Calamy's *Account*, vol. ii. p. 4t. Bishop Kennet pours great calumny on those learned divines which were appointed triers. "By the questions they were accustomed to ask," he says, "a man could not tell what they aimed at except it was in advance

Mr. Strong died in the prime of his life, and was buried in the Abbey church, July 4, 1654; but his remains were dug up at the restoration and thrown into a pit dug on purpose in St. Margaret's church-yard. This event was documented in the account given in the *Articles* of Dr. William Twisse, as well as in Strong's *Funeral Sermon.* Mr. Obadiah Sedgwick, who preached his funeral sermon, says, "That he was so plain in heart, so deep in judgment, so painful in study, so frequent, exact, and laborious in preaching, and, in a word, so eminently qualified for all the duties of the ministerial office, that he did not know his equal." Mr. Strong published several sermons and theological treatises in his life-time; and others were published after his death.

His works are, in quarto, "Thirty-one select Sermons, preached on special Occasions, by William Strong, that godly, able, and faithful Minister of Christ, lately of the Abbey at Westminster, 1656." To this volume there is a preface by Dr. Thomas Manton, Mr. John Rowe, and Mr. George Griffith. There is another preface by Dr. Henry Wilkinson, dean of Christ's Church, who gave the following account of Mr. Strong's character,

---

Quakerism, or make way for Mahometiim."—Neal's *Puritans*, vol. ii. p. 103. See also Kennet's Chronicle, p. 714.

"There is an excellent vein in his sermons, as one says in the like case, the further you search the richer treasure you are likely to find. That which made his sermons pass with so great approbation of the most judicious hearers, when he was alive, and will be a passport to his writings though posthumous, was, that he followed the advice of the Apostle to Timothy, studying to show himself approved to God, a workman that need not be ashamed, rightly dividing the word of truth. He made preaching his work. He was so much taken up in this work, that to my knowledge he was often in watchings a great part of the night, besides his pains in his day studies. But, besides that very great diligence and travail of head and heart, and that unseasonable and hard study, that he laid put in his sermons, he had a special faculty of keeping close to his text and business in hand; which, as it is very requisite in a preacher, so it is very advantageous to commend a discourse to the most judicious ear. That which further contributed to his excellency in preaching, was his skill and deep insight into the mystery of godliness, and the doctrine of the free grace of God. And as to the mystery of iniquity within us, he was well studied in the soul's anatomy, and could dexterously dissect the old man. He understood well the mystery of iniquity without us, of Satan and antichrist; and, by his knowledge of these mysteries, he was able to advance the kingdom and honor of our Lord Christ in the hearts and lives of his hearers; to discover Satan's depths, and to disappoint his plots and devices. There was one thing more which added very much unto him and to his labors in preaching, and made him successful in clearing dark places, and searching further into the deep mines of the word, and that was his constant recourse to the originals, in which he had good skill. By these means he went beyond most of his brethren in the work of the ministry; so that his sermons had always something above the ordinary reach, and a certain strain answering the advantage and happiness of the age in which he lived. There was so great a weight, both of words and sense, in this our author's sermons, and so much of worth, that they appeared as good upon a narrow disquisition as they seemed to be when they were delivered. The ignorance or want of a clear knowledge of the doctrine of the covenant of grace, God's rich and free grace in the business of our salvation, was formerly, and is still, the cause of many errors in the church. The author of these sermons had arrived to an excellency and height in this doctrine, beyond the most that I ever read or knew. Had he lived to have perfected his labors about the covenant of grace, I presume I may say they had surpassed all that went before. Though his adversaries did very much endeavor to asperse him, yet he proved them to be unjust and false. He was as happy in the purity and innocency of his life as he was for the fervor which, through grace, he erected in his preaching without fear or partiality. He was not of them who corrupt the word of God, but declared all the divine counsel. He often told me that one chief object of his study and prayer to God was, that he might be led into all truth and, teach the same both seasonably and profitably. God appointed him to labor in those places where all his abilities might be exercised and, shine forth in all their luster. Though he commonly preached four times a week, and frequently oftener, his sermons were not tilled with empty notions; but were well studied and enriched with substantial matter, the composition being close, elaborate, and pithy. And while he labored more to profit than to please, he never failed to please as well as profit those who heard him. What he delivered harmonized one part with another, and was ever supported with strong arguments. He compared spiritual things with spiritual; yet not with the enticing words of man's wisdom, but in full demonstration of the Spirit. Being filled with the Spirit, he was enabled to do much work in a little time. He did not wear out with rusting, but with using. He exhorted professors of the gospel, however they might differ about matters of discipline, to maintain good works, and bring forth the fruits of righteousness. He laboured to bring all parties to live a holy life. Indeed, he well knew that persons zealous about external matters might show with what party they sided; but by the holiness of their lives only, could they know that they were on the Lord's side. Therefore he pressed the duties of self-examination and self-denial with great earnestness and exactness, lest any persons should profess Christianity out of faction, carrying a pagan heart under a christian name."[2]

Mr. George Griffith, in his *preface* to Mr. Strong's sermons, entitled, "The Heavenly Treasure," 1656, gives the following account of the author,

"It is abundantly manifest to most of the godly through the nation, but more especially in the city of London, with what singular ability, strong affection, and good

---

[2] See Wilkinson's *Preface* to Mr. Strong's Thirty-one Sermons.

success, Mr. Strong employed and spent himself in the service of the gospel. He did the work of him who sent him while it was day; because, as he often said, the night was coming when no man can work. While he had the opportunity, neither the flatteries nor the frowns of men could hinder him from his beloved exercise. He preached the word with much freedom and boldness."

Mr. Theophilus Gale, who published Mr. Strong's "Discourse of the Two Covenants," in 1678, gives him the following account,

"He was a wonder of nature for natural parts, and a miracle of grace for deep insight into the more profound mysteries of the gospel. He had a spirit capacious and prompt, sublime and penetrant, profound and clear; a singular sagacity to pry into the more difficult texts of scripture, an incomparable dexterity to discover the secrets of corrupt nature, a divine sapience to explicate the mysteries of grace, and an exact prudence to distribute evangelical doctrines, according to the capacity of his auditors. He was a star of the first magnitude in the right hand of Christ, to diffuse the resplendent light of the gospel. And as he transcended most of this age in the explanation of evangelical truth, so, in his intelligence and explanation of the *Two Covenants*, he seems to excel himself: this being the study of his life, and that whereon his mind was mostly intent. The notices I received from his other works gave me a great impression of his divine wisdom; but what mine eyes have seen, and my thoughts imbedded of his incomparable intelligence, from his elaborate, *Discourse of the Two Covenants*, assures me, that not the half was told me by his works formerly published. He was, indeed, a person intimately and familiarly acquainted with the deepest points in theology; but especially those which relate to the covenant of grace."[3]

One of the most famous puritans, Dr. Thomas Manton, describes him as, "an eminent and a faithful servant of God, a man eloquent and mighty in the scriptures, and a burning and shining light in the church of Christ."

His works are the *following*:

1. *Thirty-one Select Sermons*, preached on special Occasions, 1656.
2. *The Heavenly Treasure*. 1656.

---

[3] Griffith's *Preface* to Mr. Strong's *Heavenly Treasure*.

3. *The Saint's Communion with God, the Saint's Privilege and Duty.* 1656.

4. *A Treatise on the Subordination of Man's Will to the Will of God,* 1657.

5. *The Eternity and Certainty of Hell's Torments,* 1672.

6. *A Discourse of the Two Covenants,* 1678.

7. *The Parable of the Prodigal (n.d.).*

DESERTION AND COMMUNION

By C. Matthew McMahon, Ph.D., Th.D.

Reader, Strong's work that you are about to read is a monument to the sweetness that the believer has in communion with Jesus Christ. There is no doubt that this work, in its faithfulness to the Scriptures, will bring you into a deeper relationship with Jesus Christ. Or, it will aid you in your examination of yourself as to whether or not God is moving *further away* than *closer to*. Strong only deals with the problem of "desertion" for just two pages. It is a real difficultly, I believe, that it is not so spoken about, and has very few treatise or papers written about, but yet, is a common problem among true Christians.

"Desertion." *Webster's Dictionary* defines the word in this manner: *Abandonment without consent*. When a man or woman desires a divorce, and they walk out on their spouse without advanced notice or communication, that is *desertion*. When a mother leaves her one month old child in the alley trash can, that is *desertion*. When a soldier defects from one country to another during the war, that is *desertion*. But does *God* desert His people? Can the same be said of Him? When *desertion* is applied to God, it is not applied in the same manner as the three illustrations above. When God deserts someone, He is not mentally incapacitated, or anxious, or in a state of sin. But it must be noted that in a very real sense, God may at times, *desert* His people. This is God's *withdrawing* of Himself in areas of empowering for service, rescuing the distraught spirit, or comforting the soul. This idea may be new to you, the reader. You may be holding onto Christ's words, "I will never leave you or forsake you." However, you have not taken into account the entirety of the Biblical picture.

Some may read this brief introduction and be distraught about such a concept. People do not realize that God may desert His people; but for reasons which may be to mysterious and incomprehensible to us, He *does*. I simply want to illustrate this point, then direct you back to Mr. Strong who will be a help to make you sure from any type of desertion – or at least point you in the right direction to gain true communion back with God. I want to briefly show how God does this, why He does this, observations about those who have been deserted, and offer some cures to dejected souls.

First, it is important to accept the reality that Scripture demonstrates examples of God's desertion to His people. A powerful illustrative passage is Isaiah 54:6-8, "For the Lord God has called you, like a woman forsaken and grieved in spirit, like a youthful wife when you were refused," says your God. "For a moment I have forsaken you, but with great mercies I will gather you. With a little wrath I hid my face from you for a moment." God may hide His face from us and forsake us for a time (*e.g.* Ps. 42:7-9, 88:6-9; 2 Cor. 4:16ff). He did this for a little time with Israel. For a moment they were *forsaken*. For a short time they were *without* His comfort, help and solace.

How or in what sense does God desert *us*? It is important to note that God may seem to have deserted someone when this is not really the case. It may be only in appearance and not really in truth. This is where people, in their emotional distress and trials, believe themselves to have been deserted by God. They may be in some desperate situation which seems insurmountable, and where they think God is not listening to their prayers or rescuing them from tribulation in a timely manner. There seems to be, (from the myopic human perspective), no deliverance in sight. Nevertheless, we must never let our *emotions* deceive our minds. Our faculty of emotions may mislead us *thoroughly*. Teenagers believe they are in love, when in fact they have no idea what love is all about. Five year olds feel as though their older siblings are more loved than they are because they get better treats or more attention from their parents. Emotions are a very tricky animal. Emotional deceptions may also manifest themselves through besetting sins in the life of a believer. This raises a feeling of doubt that God is near. Our doubt and emotions should not be allowed to overwhelm us. *They* cause us to believe that God has departed, when in fact, He is still very near. Still, sometimes, a frowning providence will draw near to us and God may in fact desert us for his own certain reasons for a time.

Desertions are not the interruptions of God's love, but an interruption in the acts of His love. When God deserts a believer, He withholds those acts of love which bless them in their spiritual growth. He never deserts us in our salvation, justification or adoption. Our salvation is secure *in Christ.* Once the eternal decree is set for our election in Christ, it is irreversible. Philippians 1:6 states, "He who began a good work in you *will continue it* until the day of Christ Jesus." Our salvation is not at risk, for we have the promises of God to stand on in this matter. But empowerment may be withheld, comfort may be neglected and the need for rescue in troublesome times may not come quickly. This is desertion for the Christian.

Though God deserts us, He never deserts us *totally.* 1 Samuel 12:22, "For the Lord will not forsake His people for His name's sake." He will never leave Israel in the wilderness. He will never allow David to live forever among the Philistines. He will not leave the Christian wandering aimlessly for all time, but He does do this sometimes for a season.

Desertions are of two kinds: 1) the withdrawing of grace, and 2) the withdrawing of comfort. When God withdraws His grace, it is not that He is taking grace out of you, but rather, He is not putting needed grace *into* you. This kind of grace would be called, "assisting or sanctifying grace." God may withhold His mercies for a time, and withdraw this grace so that the Christian hungers for it. By withholding this grace God creates a tribulation in the Christian's life. It is a tribulation of learning and teaching, for God does not desert us just for His amusement, but for specific purposes; He does this to teach us to utterly rely on Him and to remember afresh our desperate need of Him. When God withdraws comfort, it is a comfort which is needed while in tribulation. The soul is in dire need of grace because it is in a perilous situation, but God does not bring the comfort. This is when turmoil, distress, dryness, spiritual declension and complacency of the soul results because God does not comfort us as we need His everyday grace while we live in the world. This is desertion.

When God is pleased in withdrawing and refusing His grace from us, He is keeping the Spirit from further sanctifying us. But though He gives us this cup of affliction, He earnestly desires to bring us through to the end, where there is a cup of consolation. Again, God never deserts us forever. And though, on the surface, it may seem to us that it is detrimental to our sanctification to be deserted, God will ultimately use this for our greater good and his glory.

God deserts His people for very good reasons although he does not always share those reasons with us. The needs and desires of the soul are widened and enlarged in affliction. Heavenly communion with God is sweetest after an evil day, and after tribulation. It is sweetest because after the soul longs after Him for such a lengthy time, it may find all the supply and grace it lacks in the world in the Lord Christ. When people are deserted, they quickly try to fill themselves up with the *world* instead of God. When this happens, they see their need for God unlike at any other time, though this takes some time to find out. Then, they have such a hunger for Christ that the world becomes as dark and black as night. They desire it no more, and they cling to the light of Jesus Christ and His cross as the Morning Star.

The regaining of grace is a task to be taken up by a Christian who has been deserted by the Lord. There are some important observations to make about those who seek to remedy their situation. 1) There cannot be true comfort without the quickening of the Spirit of God. You will labor in vain unless the Spirit quickens you into a higher degree of grace. Without this gracious quickening, there is no cure for desertion. This may take some time, and here the Christian is to be importunate, and not to give up. Prayer than is key.

2) Sometimes, when a man is deserted, he becomes complacent about spiritual things. This is the last place you want your soul. It is a dreadful disease that takes up a hardened form of laziness and procrastination. If a soul desires to stay complacent in its desertion too long, that soul will shrivel up and wither into a sick spirit. It is so much harder to regain grace when a soul is in the state of complacency than in any other sin. Complacency sets the mind at ease in the sin and thus continues to build up more sin. It is, in and of itself, a sin. A deserted soul must wage heavy war against such thoughts and lack of action.

3) When a soul is deserted, sometimes it will not see God *as its end* when God *must be* its end. The desire of a Christian is to follow Christ. Many times a deserted soul will not see Christ after the soul has been deserted, and thus, it does not see Him as important as he once was; "you have lost your first love..." Desertion by God often moves us to sin. That does not mean God is the author of sin, but by His withdrawal or lack of comfort through grace, the soul always finds itself looking to something other than God because grace has diminished and is not seen as very important.

4) Desertions can be handled by a soul in three ways, a) hypocritically – which is when a man intends something other than what he does. Here a man will never get himself back to receiving God's grace. For his complacency makes him

hypocritical in His action. He goes to church out of duty instead of desire, and so is hypocritical in his action. b) Conscientiously a soul may try to escape his desertion. This means that the good things he needs to do (pray, read Scripture, or the like) is done out of a sense of duty instead of a sense of need. The prayer is prayed, but still, the soul is no better off than before since he is only conscientious instead of spiritual. The last sort is c) spiritual. When a man spiritually does some good, it is accomplished so they may please and enjoy God as their aim and goal. When a man enjoys walking with God, God is his whole life. Christ is his all and all. The deserted soul desires to regain lost grace again, and desires to be filled up with God.

The last observation is this, 5) those who are deserted by God often deserve to be deserted in order that they go through a time of testing for the regaining of grace again. Deserted people are those who go through a time of harsh instruction and correction by the Lord. Many times, these souls are deserted for good reason: a prideful heart, or carelessness in some besetting sin. Here, Christ allows them to experience this tribulation and this desertion for a good end, (*cf.* Romans 8:28).

Keeping these five observations in mind will help you when God deserts you for a time. There is no Christian who remains on the same level of spirituality day in and day out.

Varying degrees of grace are always at hand and desertion is not far from any one of God's children. The experience of the Shulamite woman in Song of Songs in 5:2-6 should be a constant reminder, "He knocks saying, "Open for me my sister, my love, my dove, my perfect one..." I opened for my beloved, but my beloved had turned and was gone. My heart leaped up when He spoke, I sought Him, but I could not find Him. I called Him, but He gave me no answer." Christ comes, and if we are not ready for Him, He turns and goes to another house to knock. We may search and seek for days, weeks, months, maybe even years, and still not find Him as we desire. The Shulamite was not ready, and so He left and was not found by her. But Christ is always ready to receive a soul that seeks Him in earnest.

Though we may be deserted, there are cures and remedies for this ailment of the soul. 1) Fly to prayer and the promises of God. Prayers are presenting our desires to God, and the one who is full of desires is full of prayer. Go, run quickly into your prayer closet and speak forth all your heart's desire to the Lord. Do not do this once or twice or three times, but do it until He answers without doubt. Pray without ceasing until the throne room of heaven itself resounds back to you in grace and comfort; and remember the promises of God. His word is true and steadfast. He has promised to return to you after a time. Trust with all your heart that He will fulfill His word, for He is a faithful God. Guard your mind with the Word for emotions and feelings can often shoot us down. They deceive us, where the promises build us up and make our desires into strong towers. 2) Remember that God is your end, and that you are to do all you can to make Him your end. Glorify God in your satisfaction of Him. Our desires for Him will call forth grace to rain down from heaven upon our souls. 3) Quicken your desires after God. The more you labor the more you will receive. The more you reap in Christ, the more you will sow through His grace. It is imperative that you find the cause of your desertion, which may be a sin you have committed. Find the root of that sin and despise it. Pursue your desertion to the birth of that condition and you will find a sin lying there. You may have blatantly sinned, or you may have neglected to do something God pressed you to do. Whatever it is, find the root of it and tear it from your life by the power of the Spirit of God. Many times Christians must retrace their steps back to the place of departure to get back on the road towards the Celestial City. It may be that you have *not* sinned and God simply desires to see if you *will* sin in neglecting gaining the grace He has withheld back again. Never give up! Finally, 4) It is a vain thing to think God will help you if you do not endeavor to help yourself. Christians think sanctification is a free ride. They think this until they are deserted and then find themselves scrapping for bits of grace. But if a soul desires to do the will of God with all its might, God will bring grace to his doorstep once again. You must strive to be the one who runs the race instead of being a spectator.

Desertion is a weighty matter. If you are deserted, do not stop looking for the grace of God until you have found it. The Scriptures exhort us to continue to labor in our work before God, "And let us not grow weary while doing good, for in due season we shall reap if we do not lose heart (Gal. 6:9)." And we should be constant to, "work out [our] salvation with fear and trembling (Phil. 2:12)." Our desertion is for our good; that we may once again be back into the arms of the Father. Though rain comes today, and the day is miserable, it cannot nor will not last. God will move away the clouds and allow the rays of His grace to shine through. But let Him not catch us off guard. Let us be ready before the door to open it quickly before He moves on to another house again.

Here is where William Strong comes in. He will show you how to have true communion with Christ, and what the communion is, how it is to be had, and how it is to be cultivated. May the Lord bless you as you read carefully, and study well.

C. Matthew McMahon

From my study (August, 2015)

[ORIGINAL TITLE PAGE]

The
Saints' Communion
with God
and
God's Communion
with them
in Ordinances.

As it was delivered in several sermons by that faithful servant
of Christ,
MR. WILLIAM STRONG,
late minister at Westminster.

LONDON,
Printed for *George Sawbridge* at the *Bible* on *Ludgate-hill* and
Robert Gibbs in *Chancery Lane*.
1655.

INTRODUCTORY LETTER

To his honorable friend, Colonel William Purefoy, recorder of the famous city of Coventry.

Sir,

This book, falling by providence into my hands, and the earnest entreaty of diverse Christian and pious friends in London, having drawn from me the *Epistle to the Reader*, as also having heard much of your admiration of its author, (Reverend Mr. Strong, now blessed in the eternal mansions above). I boldly commend the book also to you, as a humble acknowledgement of the faithful service I owe you, by the same way of fellowship and communion in Gospel ordinances, with the Father and his Son Jesus Christ our Lord. We must all attain to that blessed and eternal communion where the presence of God and Christ in glory shall transcend the purest ordinances here below. But if either we turn our backs on holy and precious truths received, and once publicly professed, or let our zeal cool, or by sitting still do not go forward, we both lose the comfort of communion here, and shall have less communion in glory. No doubt, sir, it is a wild age in which we live; many stupendous changes, strange turnings, and amazing alterations we have seen, both in church and state, and who knows what yet any of us must undergo. We have, therefore, more need to stick to our principles, more faithfully to own God's name and to maintain our practice in holiness with more vigor and constancy that in the end we may reap, *if we do not faint.* Which that you, sir, my honorable friend, may still perform and bring a greater glory to God and do more good to that my native city of Coventry, where I was once an unworthy lecturer, and to the whole country better service, shining more gloriously in the end of your days so that when you have finished your course with joy and kept the faith, the hour of temptation which now is on all the earth that then you may receive the crown laid up for you, which your son and wife, now both blessed and glorious, are enjoying to all eternity, is and shall be the hearty and earnest prayer of him, who does not doubt of your candid acceptation of this my bold presumption, but desires in all things ever to be found,

Sir, your most humble and faithful servant upon the best account,

JOHN HERING.

(From my study at Brides Churchyard, London.)

TO THE CHRISTIAN READER

Christian Reader,

At the earnest entreaty and request of some pious and Christian friends, who find sweet communion with God in Gospel ordinances, I boldly commend the reading of this book to you. The author, who I believe is now in heaven, received his wages after his work was done and is now a glorified saint enjoying eternal communion with God above. We must all confess that in respect of human frailties, we are not so strong, but that weakness will attend the best of us while here below in our pilgrimage to the heavenly Canaan. He will be much deceived that reckons this world his heaven, but does and will find it his wilderness, and at best, but his passage through the Red Sea. And here we have need of Moses, not only to kill the Egyptian for us, to bring us out of Egypt, to lift up his rod, to stretch forth his hand, and to divide the Red Sea that our passage may be safe, but also of Joshua to bring us into Canaan. And this is our Lord Jesus Christ, who is God blessed forevermore. No true saint in this life can live without or above ordinances, nor more than the natural body can live without food and raiment. God in his infinite wisdom and mercy has admitted the churches newborn babes in all ages to ordinances, by which grace and the seeds of regeneration may be, through mercy, conveyed to them. And saints, to the end of their days, are perfected by them also, as the apostle speaks in (Ephesians 5:26-27). Some waters are contained in springs and wells, some in conduits and pipes, and some also in the main ocean. Yet they are all conveyances of water for the several uses of the sons of men. And they are all bounded within their due limits. And so it is with Gospel ordinances— they are the wells and springs of life; they are the pipes of spiritual comfort; they are the ocean of mercy and all the privileges of free grace conveyed to the believing soul. All those in these licentious days, (which God will require somewhere), that cry down ordinances and forced themselves to devise new ways of conveying their apprehended spirit to us. And should we refuse the ways of God's own appointment? Wherever God shall record his name, shall we deny the worship of him there? How then will God come to us and bless us as he has promised? Let those wild men of this age that have been at Jericho instead of Jerusalem resolve this question: *How will the Lord appear in ways and ordinances that are not his own institution and allowance?* Will he not sadly, personally, and publically say to them at the great day: Who has required these things at your hands? Bring no more vain obligations.

Reader, I will say no more, but beseech you to turn your reading into prayer and your praying into humble and holy practice that you may know the Trinity in unity and unity in Trinity, which reason cannot understand and may enjoy soul communion with all the persons in the Trinity by faith in Gospel ordinances. And that both in the temple, and also in every administration of the Lord Jesus to you, you may cordially, affectionately, and with comfort say, *Jehovah Shammah*, the Lord is there. And with Jacob in his pilgrimage be able to confess surely the Lord is in this place, though sometimes I knew it not through mine own fault. And that you may find all mercies and glories grounded in your spiritual communion with God who is reconciled to you in Christ your Redeemer. The desire of him who thirsts after more communion with God and Christ in holy ordinances is to be founded always on a spiritual account.

Yours in the Lord Christ,

JOHN HERING.

From my study in Brides Churchyard, London, October 27, 1655.

CHAPTER 1: UNDERSTANDING THE TEXT AND DOCTRINE

"In all places where I record my name (*or where I cause my name to be remembered*) I will come unto thee, and I will bless thee," Exod. 20:24.

The whole chapter is made up of God's giving the moral law. In the giving forth of the law there are many remarkable passages. Why it must be given from Mount Sinai? Why immediately after their deliverance out of Egypt? Why in thundering and lightning? Why the world in its infancy lived without a law written? These things I have already spoken to. The words which I have read are a promise made to the places of God's public worship, which were typical, for respect to places is done away, "The hour cometh when ye shall neither in this mountain, nor yet at Jerusalem worship the Father," (John 4:21). All acts of worship are to be done to God as a Father and respect of places being done away, now children may everywhere worship their Father. The whole Jewish religion lay in these four things: (1) in holy times; (2) in holy places; (3) in holy persons; and (4) in holy things. The apostle has wrapped up a religion under the New Testament, "Pure religion and undefiled before God and the Father is this, to visit the fatherless and widows in their afflictions and keep himself unspotted from the world," (James 1:27).

Jesus Christ was made known in four ways in the Old Testament: by promises, by prophecies, by types and shadow, and by apparition. The blessing in this text comes under an apparition, for it is nothing else but the appearance of God in divine ordinances, now respect to places being done away by the promulgation of the Gospel. The promise, though it does not relate to the place, yet it does relate to the ordinances, so that in all places, if you lift up holy hands without wrath and doubting and worship the Father in Spirit, this blessing belongs to you.

In all places where I record my name—the words themselves being a promise have these particulars in them.

First, the author of it is God the Father.

Secondly, the extent of it is all places where I record my name.

Thirdly, the nature of the promise in two branches: (1) of communion—*I will come to you* and (2) of benediction—*I will bless you.*

In which you have three things:

1. The union of them—meeting and blessing

2. The order of them—first meeting and then blessing

3. The object of them (the sincere seekers of God)—I will come to you and I will bless you

There's but one thing in the text that is difficult.

In the place where *I record my name*, in the Hebrew it is

אֶת־צֹאנְךָ וְאֶת־שְׁלָמֶיךָ אֶת־עֹלֹתֶיךָ עָלָיו וְזָבַחְתָּ תַּעֲשֶׂה־לִּי אֲדָמָה מִזְבַּח

וּבֵרַכְתִּיךָ: אֵלֶיךָ אָבוֹא אֶת־שְׁמִי אַזְכִּיר אֲשֶׁר בְּכָל־הַמָּקוֹם וְאֶת־בְּקָרֶךָ

(Exod. 20:24). Transliterated for our purpose, *becol hammakom asher azker etsheni*; that is, in every place where I shall cause or make my name to be remembered, or in every place where I shall mention (or make mention) of my name. For the word אַזְכִּיר, *azkir*, is in the conjugation hiphil, which usually imports an action done or caused to be done by another, as here, *I will cause to be remembered*, the name of God has several acceptations in Scripture. By name of God is here meant the public worship and service of God, "Go ye to Shiloh, the place where I have set my name," (Jer. 7:12). So it's said, אֲשֶׁר אֶל־מְקוֹמִי לְכוּ־נָא כִּי שָׁם שְׁמֵי שִׁכַּנְתִּי אֲשֶׁר בְּשִׁילוֹ, *Jehovah echad ushemo ochad*. Jehovah shall be one and his name one, that is, he shall be worshipped as he is one in essence. In all places where I record my name I will meet you and bless you.

For the explication and confirmation of the two chief heads the text points (1) that by recording, remembering or mentioning the name of God, is meant, the setting up the worship of God in his ordinances and (2) that wherever the name of God is so recorded, remembered, or mentioned. That is, wherever God is worshipped in his ordinances, there he does promise and command a blessing; or there he will meet those that record his name in worshipping of himself with a blessing. There are two or three other parallel places of Scripture deserving special considerations. (1) For the first point, there is a most remarkable expression, (Psalm 22:27). All the nations of the world (וְיִזְבְּרוּ, *fizkeru*, the same Hebrew root with *azkir*, here in the text) shall remember. Why, what is that? Or what shall they remember? Even this, they shall turn to the Lord and the worship of him in his name and in his ordinances as is explained in the words following the verse. And all the families of the nations *jishtachavu*, shall bow down themselves, or worship before you, and so this is the meaning of Psalm 86:4. All nations whom you have made shall come *vejishtachavu*, and they shall worship before you. And how shall they do so? Even by recording, remembering, and making mention of the glory of your name as in the words following, *vicabbedu lishmecha* and they shall glorify your name. (2) For the second point, that the Lord (as he has promised, so he) does come and meet those with a blessing who does in this way glorify and worship his name in his ordinances so that they shall never do it in vain and for nothing. See those two precious texts in Isaiah's prophecy, (Isa. 45:19; 64:4-5). The incomprehensible mercies and goodness of God, which he has laid up and prepared for his people, is set forth. "Since the beginning of the world, men have not perceived by ear, neither has the eye seen," (Isa. 64:4). And then mark what follows in verse 5 where the prophet describes those who the Lord will come and meet with all those incomprehensible blessings; those who wait on him and rejoice in his worship working righteousness and remembering his name in his ways and ordinances. You meet him who rejoices and works righteousness, those who remember you in your ways. So that no less than blessings incomprehensible by the understanding and mind of man waits upon those who wait upon God and who remember his name in his worship, ways, and ordinances. And therefore, that other cited text (Isa. 45:9) is fully verified that never did any of the sons of Jacob (true Israelites) seek God (in his ways, worship, and ordinances) in vain. I did not say to the seed of Jacob you seek me in vain, or for a void or empty nothing as the word *tohu* imports. No, the sincere seekers of God in his worship and ordinances shall not be sent away with *tohu*, vacuity and emptiness, but with their cup overflowing with all the fullness of incomprehensible blessings. In this way the Lord comes and meets them with a blessing who remember his name in his worship and ordinances in all places where He records His name. I will meet you and bless you. But we are to consider that in relation to ordinances there are four sorts of men:

1. Some are altogether below ordinances.

34

2. Others are altogether above ordinances; they look on them as milk fit for babes, but not as meat fit for strong men. They look upon them as the shadows of the evening fit to be stretched over the persons whose knowledge is not very high. "We have a more sure word of prophecy where unto ye do well that he take heed, as unto a light that shineth in a dark place until the day dawn, and the daystar arise in your hearts," (2 Peter 1:19). They think that all these morning stars must go away as soon as Jesus Christ has risen as a sun in the hearts of the saints.

3. Others take up their rest in ordinances and conclude the goodness of their estate by ordinances because they have the enjoyment of ordinances; therefore, they think they have the enjoyment of God.

4. Others neither rest in, nor yet rest from, ordinances and these are persons indeed that are like to meet with a blessing when they come to God. When these come to worship him they are made welcome to him, and they shall be blessed by him. Such a spirit is fit for ordinances and such a spirit shall receive much blessing by ordinances.

The propositions that lie in the words are these:

1. One of the principal ends which God aims at the setting up of his public ordinances is that he may have communion with his saints, and that his saints may have communion with him.

2. The times of a saint's communion with God and God's communion with them are times of blessing and times of benediction.

Communion times are blessed times, and they are blessing times. Blessedness is out of the reach of the whole creation, one creature cannot make another blessed. No, all the creatures cannot make one creature blessed. Man is fallen too low for his fellow creature to advance him. He is too sore for the whole creation to make him a remedy. It's impossible for the whole creation to make any part of amends to man for the wrong that he did himself. Creatures cannot take off that curse which they lie under themselves. How then can they give the blessing that's lacking to others? Nothing is able to work or move above what it is in *being*. The world in its being is poor and beggarly; therefore, it can never make us rich. "I will hear that heavens, and they shall hear the earth," (Hos. 2:21). The heavens cry to God; the earth cries to the heavens; the creatures cry to the earth. Still we are led up the stairs by one creature to another, until we have passed through them all to God himself, and in this indeed does our blessedness lie. Creatures want blessedness for themselves. How can they give blessedness to us?

3. The DOCTRINE that might be raised from the words: *That the foundation of all the blessedness of man is the will of*

God. I will meet them and bless them. But it's the first of these I shall speak of.

That one of the principal ends which God aims at in setting up his public ordinances is that he may have communion with the saints and that his saints might have communion with him.

While every man lives here is at a distance from God. There's a two-fold distance that is between God and the creatures: First, a distance in point of reconciliation, and secondly, a distance in point of communion. There's a natural distance as we are creatures and a moral distance as we are sinners. I shall premise three things: (1) The Scripture holds forth such a state; (2) The communion that the saints have with God is with all persons in the Trinity; (3) The communion in this life is chiefly in ordinances.

The first position: That the Scripture holds forth such a state of communion between God and his people such as is between the bride and the bridegroom in the bride chamber. It's true I confess all godliness is a mystery, "Great is the mystery of godliness," (1 Tim. 3:16), but yet in this there are some mysteries greater than others. Observe, there is such an intimacy spoken of, "Our fellowship is with the Father and with his Son Jesus Christ," (1 John 1:3). Then the saints have a fellowship with the Father and with Christ, yet notwithstanding some of them have a more peculiar fellowship with God than others. It's true; whosoever he is that is taken into union is taken into communion too. All the saints who have a communion with themselves have a communion with Christ also, for they do all meet as one with him, as lines meet in the center. Yet there are some saints in this life who have a more peculiar communion with the Lord than others. God says, "If there is a prophet I will speak to him in a dream, in a vision, but my servant Moses (it's not so with him), I will speak to him mouth to mouth as a man to his friend, and the similitude of God shall he behold," (Num. 12:8). He shall have such discoveries of God as ordinary saints do not have; he shall have such communion with God as ordinary believers do not have.

Now this communion of God with the saints will appear to be a very great and glorious intimacy and familiarity, if you look to the several denominations that are given to them in the Scripture, all of them imply a very great familiarity, *as:*

1. They are called his friends. "Abraham was called the friend of God," (James 2:23). "I have not called you servants, but I have called you friends," (John 15:16). And as Jesus Christ calls them friends, so they call him friend too. "This is my beloved, and this is my friend O daughters of Jerusalem," (Song of Solomon 5:6). What is a friend? Truly it is a man's own self, "Thy friend which is as thine own soul," (Deut. 13:6).

Then friendship speaks of high familiarity. Augustine speaks of himself concerning a friend of his who died—he professed he was put into a great straight, whether he himself should be willing to live or will to die. He was unwilling to live because one half of him was dead, yet he was not willing to die because his friend did partly live in him though he was dead.

2. He calls the church the bride, the Lamb's wife. There is the same resemblance between Christ and his church, as between man and wife. Now you know husband and wife become one flesh so that this matrimonial union is but a shadow and resemblance of the glorious union that is between Christ and his church. There is a great deal of intimacy between man and his wife; therefore, she is called, "the wife of his bosom," (Deut. 6:3). Now what is the *bosom*? It's the seat of secrecy and the seat of intimacy. For this cause the Lord Jesus Christ is said to be in the, "bosom of the Father," (John 1:18), as one that is acquainted with all his secrets and as one that enjoys the most intimate familiarity with the Father. So you are the wife of the bosom of Christ. This I think to be the meaning of that. It is said, "Lazarus died and was carried into Abraham's bosom," (Luke 16:23). Dives (*the Rich Man*) when he died was in the torments of hell. Surely then the other was in heaven. Why is it called Abraham's bosom? It is a place of rest and a place of love. All the saints being Abraham's children are of Abraham's covenant and promise. They are received into

Abraham's bosom in glory with a great deal of love and are taken into his bosom as into the resting place. In this way the children of God stand in the same relation to Christ as a wife to the husband.

3. There is yet a higher expression of intimacy than this. All these are but external and fleshly, but the union of the Spirit is much stronger. "He that is joined to the Lord is one Spirit," (1 Cor. 6:17). He that is joined to the flesh is one flesh, but he that is joined to the Lord is one Spirit. It's as if there was a union of two souls. Cyprian, when he would express this union, says it's a union of walls and a confederacy of affections; they grow into one spirit. These relations do import this much, for the Lord Jesus Christ does not give empty titles.

It will further appear if you consider those high acts of intimacy that the Scripture speaks of. I will name four:

(1) Christ and his people are said to walk together: Christ, "walks in them," (Rev. 2:1); "he walks among them," (2 Cor. 6:16). And we read of, "galleries in which the king is held," (Song of Solomon 7:5). What are those galleries? They are places of intimate converse where friends walk together and enjoy communion one with another. Now, "can two walk together except they are agreed?" (Amos 3:3). Walking implies intimacy and familiarity.

(2) They sup together. Now to eat and to drink together in Scripture is an expression of great familiarity; and therefore, the apostle says, "with such a one eat not," (1 Cor. 5:11); that is withdrawing familiarity. Not to eat with one is an argument of withdrawing familiarity, but to eat together is an argument of familiarity. "I will come to him and sup with him, and he with me," (Rev. 3:21). And for this cause when the communion of saints is set forth, it is set forth by eating and drinking together at the same table, "We being many are one bread and one body," (1 Cor. 10:17). We are many in number, (as Erasmus has it), but by the consent of our spirits, we become one bread. When the Lord would express the intimacy the saints have with him, then he is said to sup with them and they with him and mark how he does cheer him up, "Eat O friends, drink ye, drink ye abundantly O ye beloved," (Song of Solomon 5:1).

(3) They do not only sup together, but they dwell together. "Christ dwells in your hearts by faith," (Eph. 3:17). It is the great command the Lord lays upon the husband: He must dwell with his wife. Now if Jesus Christ will undertake the relation of a husband, he must dwell with his spouse. He tells you he will fulfill his relation, "I will come to you and make my abode with you," (John 14:23). As if the Lord could never speak enough, "I will dwell in them, and I will wake among them," (2 Cor. 6:16).

(4) They do not only dwell together, but they lie together: Christ and his people lie in one bed. "Our bed is green," (Song of Solomon 1:16). It's not *grarseni*, my bed, but *grarsenu*, our bed. What is that? Truly they are those ordinances of worship in which the Lord together with his people does exercise those high acts of intimacy and familiarity. "Thou settest thy bed upon a high mountain and, thither thou wentest up to offer sacrifices; thou hast enlarged thy bed," (Isa. 7:8). What is that? Florelius says the place was for idolatrous worship, in which they did commit spiritual adultery. Now the Lord deems idolatrous ordinances the bed of idols. On the other hand, the bed in which the Lord Christ and his people enjoy intimacy and familiarity is the bed of ordinances. And for this cause the church glories in this, "He shall lie all night between my breasts," (Song of Solomon 1:13). So much for the first thing I promised, namely, that the Scripture holds forth such a state of communion between God and his people. I shall but name the other two and so pass on.

The second position: The communion that the saints have with God is with all the persons. They have not only communion with the Father, but communion with the Son and not only communion with the Son, but also with the Spirit. With all persons in the Trinity, the people of God have communion. "Truly our fellowship is with the Father and his Son Jesus Christ," (1 John 1:3).

The third position: The communion in this life is chiefly in ordinances, for the immediate communion is reserved for another world. All of the communion we have in this world is a mediate communion. There are mediums between us and God through which God conveys grace to us and draws us up to him. Ordinances are the galleries. There is a wall of sin, and there are the windows of ordinances. He stands behind our wall of sin, but he looks through the windows of ordinances.

1. Let me prove it from Scripture which expresses the end that God aims at by setting up his ordinances. He might have communion with the saints and his saints have communion with him. When God comes to reform his ordinances and to purge his church, "I heard a great voice saying, behold the tabernacle of God is with men, and he will dwell with them," (Rev. 21:3). The tabernacle and temple were places of public worship. It was his dwelling and his walking with them. Dwelling notes constancy and walking notes familiarity. He will be constant and he will be familiar with his people in ordinances. "And the name of the city shall be, the Lord is there," (Ezek. 48:35). It's a prophecy that receives its accomplishment, when Jews and Gentiles shall be brought to worship God. Now when these two shall be made one in the hand of the Lord, then shall the name of the city be called *Jehovah shaumah*, that is, the Lord is here.

2. Proof: This has been the great ground of all the preparations that the saints have made. When, they have approached God in ordinances that they might have communion with God in them. "The Lord pardons everyone that prepares his heart to seek God, though not according to the purification of the sanctuary," (2 Chron. 30:18). As a bride prepares herself for her bridegroom, so do the saints prepare to meet with God in ordinances, they trim up their lamps to meet the bridegroom. "Let us draw near," (Heb. 10:22). "Awake, O north wind, and come thou south, blow upon my garden that the spices thereof may blow out; let my beloved come into his garden and eat his pleasant fruit," (Song of Solomon 4:16). They begged a north wind for ripening and the south wind for refreshing of all their fruits. But for what end? For no other, but that her beloved might come into his garden and that he might taste his pleasant fruit.

3. Proof: The end why God sets up his ordinances among a people to whom he will show mercy is certainly that he will meet with them and have communion with them in these ordinances. For God to withdraw his fellowship and communion when the saints of God are in acts of worship before him, is threatened as one of the greatest judgments "They shall go with their flocks and herds to seek the Lord, but they shall not find him for he hath withdrawn himself from them," (Hosea 5:6). That is, they should go to acts of

public worship, but they should enjoy no communion, or society, and no fellowship with God, for he had withdrawn himself from them. When they drew near to him, he should draw back from them. He should leave them to the naked use of the ordinances which was one of the greatest curses in the world. Alas, what sap or sweetness can be found in an ordinance that is appointed by God, if God himself who is the sweetness of all ordinances be withdrawn from them? Therefore, then do these positions clearly follow.

(1) Position: In all these ordinances in which you come before God and do not meet with him, they are all in vain. To converse with ordinances and not to converse with God, to have to do with ordinances and not to have to do with God. Alas, they are but dry breasts and a miscarrying womb that will never bring forth the fruits of holiness. Ordinances without God are like bones that have no marrow in them; they are like shells without a kernel. Your hearing will be vain and your hearing will be in vain. Your praying will be vain and your praying will be in vain. There will be no spirit moving, no voice answering, no heartwarming, no soul refreshing, and no God meeting. It's a sad thing for God to do these two things: *First*, to leave ordinances to men, and second, to leave these men to these naked ordinances. The poor man at the pool of Bethsaida lay there long, and longer he might have lain if Jesus Christ had not come and given cure to him. There are three

things in ordinances when they become effectual: There is majesty, sweetness, and power.

First, majesty and glory is discovered, "We all with open face behold as in a glass the glory of the Lord are changed into the same image," (2 Cor. 3:18). What's that? The glass is Gospel ordinances. They are the windows by which we look into the glory of God. Alas, without this, preaching is but babbling; praying is but howling. It's not the ordinances that put a glory upon God, but it is God that puts a glory upon ordinances. What is it that puts a beauty and glory upon all the ordinances of God? It's the presence of God; the very presence of God that makes all glory in heaven and in the church. *Jehovah Shammah*, the Lord is there is the glory of all ordinances. Yet if you do not have God in them, you may say as she said the glory is departed. They are but like the beams that are cut off from the sun, if God is not in them. Thus there is majesty and glory discovered.

Secondly, there's sweetness that the soul tastes in ordinances, but when the soul lacks the presence of God in ordinances, then there is no sweetness in them. For ordinances to the soul when the presence of God is departed from them carry no more taste or sweetness in them than is in the white of an egg. The word is sweeter than the honey and the honeycomb when God is in it. What is it that gives a soul sweetness of taste in any ordinance? "I sat under his shadow with great delight, and his fruit was sweet unto my taste," (Song of Solomon 2:3). (The word is very significant, for it imports sweetness or all kind of sweetness; his fruit was מָתִק, *mamtakkim*, all sweetness.) What's the reason men grow weary of ordinances? It's because they taste no sweetness in them? What's the reason they taste no sweetness in them? It's because God is withdrawn from them.

Thirdly, there must not only be majesty and glory discovered and sweetness tasted, but there must also be a power felt for ordinances to do you any good. "Who hath believed our report?" (Isa. 55:1). Why? They had made reports to be believed, but none had believed the reports that were made—many hearers but few believers. It's spoken by way of complaint: Who has believed our report? Why? What's the ground that the report is not believed? To whom is the arm of the Lord revealed? If the arm of God is not revealed, reports of God won't be believed. The apostle Paul says, "I am not ashamed of the Gospel of Christ, for it's the power of God to salvation," (Rom. 1:16). So the weapons of our warfare are not carnal but mighty. Mighty? How? Through God, for the bringing down of every lust that exalts itself against him. If God is not in an ordinance, the ordinance is of no effect.

CHAPTER 2: PERFECTED COMMUNION

(2) Position: That when communion with God shall be perfected and completed, then all ordinances shall be abolished and removed. Ordinances shall be continued until our communion is perfected, until we all come, "in the unity of the faith, and of the knowledge of the Son of God to a perfect man, unto the measure of the stature of the fullness of Christ," (Eph. 4:13). When once we are brought to a perfect man in Christ Jesus, then, and not until then, shall all ordinances be taken from us. In the state of our perfection God will do these two things: *First*, he will succeed all ordinances, and second, he will exceed all ordinances. All our veils shall then be taken away when we come to look God in the face. "Until the daybreak, and the shadows flee away, turn beloved, and be thou like a roe, or a young hart upon the mountains of Bether," (Song of Solomon 2:17). Some expound it of the night of troubles and of miseries that the church of God lay under; others of the obscurity and darkness that was upon them; others of those ceremonies and shadows that they could not see through; others of the coming of the Lord Jesus Christ as the sun into the world to make day, to the daybreak; others of Christ's last appearance removing all clouds and veils and causing the day to break forth and the shadow to fly away.

When, once the communion of the saints of God shall be perfected then all ordinances shall be removed, the substance shall succeed and exceed the shadows. In this way communion with God in ordinances shall last until Jesus Christ makes a surrender of his mediatorial kingdom, when Jesus Christ shall give up his kingdom to his Father, and all the saints shall be perfected, then their communion with God through mediums shall be done away.

CHAPTER 3: PURE ORDINANCES

(3) Position: The more spiritual and pure any ordinances are the more communion the saints of God have with God in them. Under the Law they lay under more carnal administrations and ordinances; and therefore, Hebrews 9:10. They are called carnal ordinances. For the most part they had but transient, not constant, acts of communion with God. These acts of communion they had but seldom, compared with those acts of communion that the saints have under the Gospel. Now as the ordinances grow up in purity and perfection, so should we grow up in communion with God in them. For the more spiritual the ordinances are, the more there is of these three things in them: 1. There's more of the nature of God in them. 2. There's more of the presence of God with them. 3. There's more of the blessing of God upon them. The ground of God's withdrawing and departing from ordinances has been men's intolerable corrupting and defiling of them so that he would neither own the worship nor the worshippers at all. "Who walketh in the midst of the seven golden candlesticks," (Rev. 2:1); if the candlesticks are gold, and there is no dross in them, then he will walk in the midst of them; but if they are dross and not golden candlesticks, God takes no delight to walk among such. "My beloved feeds

among the lilies," (Song of Solomon 2:16). It is not said he feeds among thorns, but he feeds among the lilies.

CHAPTER 4: UNREGENERATE MEN HAVE NO FELLOWSHIP WITH GOD

But for the further clearing of the saint's communion with God, I shall do these four things:

1. Give you the grounds of all the fellowship and the communion that the saints have with God in ordinances.

2. Show you the properties of this communion.

3. The several acts of communion.

4. Those glorious ends that God aimed at in the giving forth communion to the saints in ordinances.

But before I enter upon these, I must promise some few particulars.

Objection: It will be said, God is in heaven and the saints are upon the earth. God is a consuming fire, and we are but as withered stubble. How shall we draw near to God or appear before him?

Answer: There are two sorts of people in the world: First, sinners or unregenerate men; second, saints or regenerate men. They are both called on to draw near to God. "Draw nigh to God, and he will draw nigh to you: cleanse your hands ye sinners and purify your hearts ye double minded: observe those three things," (James 4:8).

(1) Here's a duty enjoined; drawing nigh to God.

(2) A blessing promised; he will draw nigh to you.

(3) There is a three-fold duplicity mentioned: sinners and double-minded; cleanse and purify hands and heart.

The first shows the persons to whom the duty is enjoined to draw near to God: the sinners and double-minded. The other two points are the way and means by which the duty enjoined may be rightly accomplished by cleansing and purifying our hearts and hands.

But it is to be marked that there is a two-fold drawing nigh to God: (1) in point of conversion and (2) in point of communion.

So that you that enjoy ordinances and are not converted, you can have no communion with God in ordinances. And for the proof of this, those unregenerate men can have no communion with God in ordinances, will appear by these arguments.

1. Because there must be a state of communion before there can be any acts of communion. There must be a state of marriage before there is a performance of the acts of the married. You must be made near before you can draw near, "Ye who were sometimes afar off are made nigh by the blood of Jesus," (Eph. 2:13). When once a soul is made nigh, then it can draw nigh. The prodigal son is returned home to the house of his father and made nigh to him, then the father

"kisses him and embraces him," (Luke 15:20). Love is very quick sighted; he saw him and was very tenderhearted. He had compassion on him and fell upon his neck and kissed him. You will see what a man is in his natural estate, which clearly speaks he has no communion with God. "That at that time ye were without Christ, being aliens from the common-wealth of Israel and strangers from the covenants of promise, having no hope, and without God in the world," (Eph. 2:12). There are five: without Christ, without the church, without the promise, without hope, and without God in the world. Can two walk together except they are agreed? God and a sinner are not agreed; there's no walking together. Therefore, a man must be made a free man before he can trade as a freeman. So before you can have any intercourse with heaven or any free trading there, you must be made free of the city above.

2. An unregenerate man can have no communion with God in ordinances because he does not live the same kind of life that God lives. No creature can have any fellowship or communion with God, but he that lives the same kind of life with God. A man cannot have communion with beasts. Why? Because they do not live a rational life, "having their understandings darkened, being alienated from the life of God," (Eph. 4:18). No things have any communion, but only those that live the same kind of life with that with which they have communion. A saint that lives the same kind of life with

God though he does not have the same degree of life with God.

3. Argument: An unregenerate man can have no fellowship with God in ordinances because he is swallowed up with other fellowship and with other communions. There is a five-fold fellowship and communion that an unregenerate man has that makes him have no communion with God.

(1) He takes up his fellowship and communion with sin. Sin is the only jewel that he wears in his bosom. "What fellowship hath Christ with Belial?" (2 Cor. 6:15-16), and, "The carnal mind is enmity against God," (Rom. 8:7). Enmity is the highest degree of hatred. It's the affection set on edge against God. An enemy may be reconciled, but enmity must be destroyed. What fellowship can they have with the Father of lights, whose fellowship is taken up with the works of darkness?

(2) They are swallowed up with the fellowship and communion with sinners. Those that are God's professed enemies are their bosom friends; the darling delights of their souls are in the society of those in whom God takes no pleasure, nor any delight.

(3) They take up their fellowship and communion with this world. "Know ye not that the friendship of the world is enmity with God?" (James 4:4). Whoever, therefore, will be a friend of the world is the enemy of God. They make

up their heaven upon earth. There are three things in which they go out to the world: 1. They let out their choicest love. 2. They lay out their choicest plans. 3. They anchor their greatest hopes on the world. Now those that are taken up with the fellowship and communion with this world, at what distance do they stand from communion and fellowship with God? Creatures have their hearts; God does not have them. 4. They are swallowed up in communion and fellowship with false foundations. This is a certain rule: Look at the foundation that we built our souls upon; that's what we have communion with. "He shall lean upon his house, but it shall not stand," (Job 8:14). Those hopes that it has are that it shall go well with him to all eternity. These are called his house. He rests upon them, and he has communion with them. Houses are (1) dwelling places—a man lives in his house, (2) hiding places— in the time of a storm, men retire to their houses for shelter, (3) resting places, and (4) places that when once they are built, men will keep them, if they can, from falling down. Now sinners are swallowed up in communion and fellowship with those false bottomed hopes that they have laid their souls upon. They rest in those houses that they make to themselves, though their hopes are but like spider's webs, yet they lean on their houses. 5. They are swallowed up in fellowship and communion with the very devil himself. "We know that we are of God, and that the whole world lies in wickedness," (1

John 5:19). In the Greek it's this: the whole world lies in that wicked one, the devil, and they maintain communion together. The evil spirits haunt their spirits. The devil in Scripture is said to have all those acts of worship performed to him by sinners that Christ is said to have performed to him by saints. Has Jesus Christ his ministers? The devil has his ministers also; ministers of Satan transforming themselves into angels of light. Has Christ his churches? So has the devil, which is called *the synagogue of Satan*. Has Christ his ordinances and altars? So has the devil too; he has his table and his communicants. You cannot be partakers of the Lord's Table and the table of the devil.

(4) The fourth argument to prove that unregenerate men can have no fellowship and communion with God in ordinances is because they live under a legal covenant. Evangelical communion is not grounded upon legal covenants. In conversion there is a double change: 1. a change of a man's nature that is wrought within him, and 2. a change of a man's state that is wrought upon him. Every unregenerate man is under the first Covenant, which admits of no communion with God since it is broken. There are five things we lost in the fall: 1. our holy image and became vile; 2. our Son-ship and became slaves; 3. our friendship and became enemies; 4. our communion and became strangers; and 5. our glory and became miserable. Now it's impossible that sinners without

the help of God are translated from a broken *Covenant of Works* made with them in Adam to a *Covenant of Grace* that is made with Christ that they should come up to communion with God. It is not something that automatically happens from one age or dispensation to the next. You must know that communion with God is *not a legal dispensation*; and therefore, every person that is duly under the Law cannot enjoy communion with God because they remain under the law until God moves them into his grace.

CHAPTER 5: THE GROUND OF THE SAINT'S FELLOWSHIP

Having premised these, I come to those four particulars I laid down, to give you the grounds, the properties, the acts, and the ends of the communion.

First, for the ground of all the fellowship and communion that the saints have with God in ordinances. They are five, for this communion arises:

1. From his electing love.

2. From the covenant state in which believers stand.

3. From our union with Jesus Christ.

4. From our interest in the Spirit.

5. From our conformity to the Lord Jesus Christ.

The ground of our communion with God is his electing love. That's the foundation of all our blessedness and the only spring of all our mercies which without God's electing love, no mercy would be a mercy to us, and with it no misery will make us miserable. The Lord has chosen you to three great ends in subordination one to the other. He has chosen you to salvation, to reconciliation, and to communion. "The Lord hath set apart him that is godly for himself," (Psalm 4:3). God has picked and culled every godly man out of the world and set him aside. For what? For himself. For himself? What's that? It does not only note for spiritual service, but for the highest privileges. He has set the godly man apart for these two ends: First, for the enjoyment of communion with him on earth, and second, for the fruition of blessedness with him in heaven. The Lord has set apart the godly.

1. Consider who it is that has done it? It's God that has set him apart.

2. What has he done? He has set him apart and put him distinct from the entire world.

3. Who is it that is thus set apart? It is the man that is godly.

4. What is the end of this action for which this man is set apart? He is set apart for God.

It's the choicest duty that belongs to us to set ourselves apart for God, and it's one of the choicest mercies of God, to set us apart for himself. The Lord separates to himself for employment and for fellowship. He will employ that man, and he will have communion with that man. The angels are of all creatures taken to special communion with God. They behold the face of God the Father which is in heaven. It was excellently expressed by Tertullian that saints in this life are the men that are the Lord's attendants who set the Lord always before them, stand always before him, and wait on him. "Thus saith the Lord, if thou wilt walk in my ways, I will give thee *mah-lechim*," (Zech. 3:7), "walks,"—that is, places to walk. *Ben hagnomedim hal-elleh, inter stantes illos,* בֵּין מַהְלְכִים לְךָ וְנָתַתִּי

הָאֵלֶּה הָעֹמְדִים, or among these that stand by. Who are they? The meaning is conceived to be this: the angels always stand before God; a thousand thousands compass his throne. Now when the Lord speaks of taking a people into intimate familiarity with himself, he says he will give them *walks*, or galleries, to walk among the angels themselves, to attend upon him, and here are those and such like expressions of this their office and duty. I have set the Lord always before me, and as the eyes of servants are upon the hands of their masters, and as the eyes of a waiting maid to the hand of her mistress, so our eyes are on the Lord our God, (waiting) until he has mercy on us. Now had the Lord chose you but to salvation, when he left the angels to fall under the curse of their covenant broken, this had been a great mercy. But this will not satisfy electing love, only to make up old breaches, and then to shut up its bosom. Or to say to us, as David said to Absalom, let him never see my face. No, but God will have his children look him in the face; therefore, there is not only, "glory to God in the highest and peace on earth," (Luke 2:14), which is reconciliation, but also there is, "goodwill towards men," (Luke 2:14). There is fellowship and communion. Peace will not serve love's turn, but there must be goodwill too. The love of God ordained us to fellowship. The Father in love came forth from all eternity to us that we to all eternity might enjoy communion with him. I had almost said that the very essence of the love of God, and all the actings of it, lead to communion and fellowship with him.

The second ground of communion is from the Covenant of Grace under which you stand. When Adam had sinned, he ran away from God. When he made himself a sinner, God made him an exile. Now in the Covenant under which Adam was, he had communion with God as a creature with his Creator, but not as a child with his father. Now the Covenant of Grace is a conjugal covenant. And conjugal covenants are all made for the enjoying of communion. "I will betroth thee to me forever; yes, I will betroth thee unto me in righteousness, and in judgment, and in loving kindness, and in mercies," (Hosea 2:19). Make note here, there are four things in these words that point out the firmness and the stability of our marriage with Christ: First, it's done in righteousness, second, in judgment, third, in loving kindness, and fourth, in tender mercies. Now what are the fruits and effects of this same conjugal relation and of our joining to Christ? "And I said, thou shalt be for me many days and shalt not be for another, so will I be for thee," (Hosea 3:3). Christ promises to be for the saints, and he engages the saints to be for him. "Strangers to the covenant of promise, without God and without hope in the world," (Eph. 2:12), until such a time as a man is brought into covenant with God, he is a stranger to God; and therefore, has no communion with him. He stands at the greatest distance from this fellowship with the Father and with his Son Jesus Christ. But now, when a man is brought within the verge of the Covenant of Grace, then he has communion in all the grace of the Covenant. The Covenant of Grace has two properties peculiar to it, which were not in the first covenant. First, there is *foedus amicitiae and fodus conjugale; a covenant of friendship* and *a conjugal covenant.* This is the great end of the Gospel. The angels described the purpose of God, and what is it? "To give peace on earth and goodwill," (Luke 2:14): God contents himself not only with peace, but also with goodwill; not only reconciliation, but also communion. And the Lord delights that his people should come to him in a familiar way, under terms of intimacy. The Lord says, "Thou shalt not call me Ishi and shalt call me no more Baali," (Hos. 2:16). *Baali* signifies *my Lord.* God would be called Lord no more, but called Ishi. What's that? *My husband.*

The third ground of communion of saints with God is their union with Jesus Christ. Answerable to your union, there will be your communion. There's a five-fold union:

1. A union political as between a king and his people.

2. A union natural as between head and members.

3. A union sinful as between one sinner and another.

4. A union hypostatical as between the two natures of Christ.

5. A union mystical as between Christ and the saints.

The righteousness that Christ has as Mediator is yours. And the communion that Christ has with the Father, we have interest in also, "For as the body is one and hath many members, and all the members of that one body being many, are one body, so also is Christ," (1 Cor. 12:12). God the Father never looks on Christ and the saints as two, but as one. Will you take a view of Christ's communion with the Father? "I saw and behold one like the Son of man came with the clouds of heaven and came to the ancient of days, and they brought him near before him," (Dan. 7:13). "He lives in the bosom of the Father," (John 1:18).

Now in his communion with the Father, we are in no less than the whole of our salvation interested. For he is brought before the Father standing at his right hand and lying in his bosom, not only to enjoy communion with his Father himself, but also to intercede for our communion with him also.

Union that disposes for communion; there can be no communion where there is no union. "Behold I stand at the door and knock, if any man hear my voice, and open the door, I will come in to him, and will sup with him, and he with me," (Rev. 3:20). First, there must be the opening of the door, and Jesus Christ must come in before there is supping together. And there is no fare for the feast when a Christian comes until Christ himself brings it. If the door is shut against Christ's person, then there is a barricade to all communion. "I am come into my garden, my sister, my spouse; eat my friends, drink, yes, drink abundantly, O beloved," (Song of Solomon 5:5). There are two things that we enjoy by virtue of our union with Christ: First, satisfaction in him, and second, communion and fellowship with him. Look what fellowship and communion Christ has with the Father. It is by virtue of his union with him and what fellowship and communion we have with Christ. It's by virtue of our union with him. Mark how the relation there arises, "All are yours; how comes that? Ye are Christ's, and Christ's is God's," (1 Cor. 3:22-23); "by whom we have access into this grace wherein we stand," (Rom. 5:2). Note *this:*

1. Believers have under the Gospel access into glorious grace; into his grace.

2. That the meritorious cause of believers' access into this grace is the Lord Jesus Christ; by *whom:*

3. The same state of grace to which the Gospel brings us, in that estate Christ keeps us; this is where we *stand:*

4. That a saint through the sight of his access to, and his standing in this grace, is made to rejoice in hope of the glory of God, as is expressed in the words following for clearing and confirmation of the substance of all those four particulars. That believers have access to and are kept to that state of grace in which they rejoice and glory, only by Jesus

Christ and his mediation there is a remarkable expression of the apostle, "But now in Christ Jesus, ye who sometimes were far off, are made nigh by the blood of Jesus; for he is our peace, who hath made both one, and hath broken down the middle wall of partition," (Eph. 2:13). Those who are without Christ are afar off in three ways: (1) in point of opinion and apprehension, (2) in point of fellowship and communion, and (3) in point of grace and conversion. Now as Joseph said to his brothers bring your brother Benjamin with you, or else do not see my face anymore. So God says this to sinners when they come near to enjoy communion with him, *bring Jesus Christ in your arms, or else never look me in the face.* It's the custom of some countries and foreign nations that whenever they speak anything to the king, they take up his son in their arms. I am sure it's the custom of heaven that whoever shall have communion with God and enjoy fellowship with his Spirit must take his Son in their arms and carry Christ along with them. "Let us therefore come boldly to the throne of grace that we may obtain mercy and find grace to help in time of need," (Heb. 4:16). God has set up a throne and that throne he has set up is a gracious throne. And it is set up for poor sinners and for poor sinners to come freely and boldly to take liberty in speaking to God. It is set up for these two ends: for the obtaining of mercy and for the finding of grace that may help us in the time of need. That is for the findings of favor and fellowship with God. And it is upon this account alone of the Lord Jesus Christ that we can come with boldness to it. Look on the words, "For we have not a high priest that cannot be touched with the feeling of our infirmities. Let us therefore come boldly," (Heb. 4:15), and, "I am the way, the truth, and the life," (John 14:6). There is no coming to the Father but by Jesus Christ. "Having therefore brethren, boldness to enter into the holiest by the blood of Jesus," (Heb. 10:19). The sinful wretches in the world, if they are brought to Jesus Christ, may come boldly and have communion with God the Father. "The king hath brought me into his chambers," (Song of Solomon 1:4). There is no going into the chambers, the places of communion with God the Father, but by being led by the hand of the King of saints, the Lord Jesus Christ to that place.

The fourth ground of our communion with God is the Spirit of Christ in us. This is one of the main ends why believers receive the Spirit of Christ. The Spirit of Christ is not only received as a bond of union, but as a means of communion, the Spirit of Christ in believers has these four things in it: It's a Spirit of union, unction, action, and fellowship.

1. It's a Spirit of union. It is the everlasting tie of the Godhead in itself. The Spirit running forth through the Father and the Son, or proceeding from the Father and the Son, as it is expressed in the Gospel. So it's the very tie and knot of the

saints and Christ. "He that is joined to the Lord is one Spirit," (1 Cor. 6:17).

2. It's a Spirit of unction; "but the anointing which ye have received abideth in you," (1 John 2:27). The ointment that was poured on the head of Aaron ran down to the skirts of his entire garment. The Spirit of God is like an ointment that was poured forth on the head of Christ, and it does run down to all his members.

3. It's a Spirit of action; the apostle says, "if ye through the Spirit mortify the deeds of the flesh," (Rom. 8:13). The Spirit is the most powerful weapon in our hands to put flesh to death in us. It is not an idle, but an active Spirit.

4. It's a Spirit of fellowship and communion. "For through him we both have an access by one Spirit unto the Father," (Eph. 2:18). We both, Jew and Gentile, have access. Though they are two nations one Spirit leads them both to the Father. The Spirit of Christ is not only a Spirit of manifestation and of revelation, but it is also a Spirit of supplication and of leading. It leads us by the hand to the Father. "As many as are led by the Spirit of God, they are the Sons of God," (Rom. 8:14).

In this way you see that intimacy is grounded on your union with Christ. The ground of all communion is union. Now answerable to the union we have, the communion must be a union which is very near, for truly the communion must be very intimate. "We are of his flesh and of his bone, he that is joined to the Lord is one Spirit," (Eph. 5:3); it is so near—no, nearer. What's the end why the Lord has made so near a union? Truly it is that there may be an intimate communion answerable. He is in us like leaven, even as the leaven incorporates itself that there can be no separation between it and the dough. One end of the hypostatical union was the mystical union; Christ takes the two natures into one person so that you might become one with him. Consider there is a moral union that is made by love, for love is *affectu unionis*, a uniting the angels have, and Adam had in the state of innocence. But there is likewise a union that faith makes, a mystical union that is another kind of union than even the angels had or can have. The angels are never said to be the brothers of Christ and the members of Christ. Christ is said to be their head, but they are never said to be his members. There is something more in that mystical union which is by faith between Christ and believers than there can be in that union which is between Christ and the angels. Now if the end of union is communion, why has the Lord made it such a close union, but for an *intimate* familiarity and communion?

The fifth ground of communion is our conformity and similitude to Jesus Christ. Conformity and similitude is the ground of all communion. A saint being made like to God receives communion and fellowship with God, the more a

Christian grows up into conformity with God, the higher he grows in his fellowship and communion with God. The less any man has of a divine resemblance, the less he enjoys of a divine communion. When our images shall be perfected, then our communion shall be completed. The more imperfect our image is, the more imperfect our communion is. I shall lay down two propositions: (1) that a saint has conformity and a resemblance of God upon him, and (2) that his conformity and resemblance to God is the ground of his communion with God.

1. That a saint has conformity and a resemblance of God upon him. "For as he is, so are we in this world," (1 John 4:17); "Whereby are given unto us, exceeding great and precious promises that by them we may be made partakers of the divine nature," (2 Peter 1:4). There's a kind of impression of the glorious attributes of God stamped on every Christian.

(1) There's a kind of omnipotency, "I can do all things through Christ that strengthens me," (Phil. 4:13). What can omnipotency do more than all things? And yet Paul can do no less by the strength he receives from Christ.

(2) There's a kind of omnisciency in all the saints, "But ye have an unction from the holy one, and ye know all things," (1 John 2:20). There are some footsteps of that glorious attribute of God that are to be seen upon gracious souls. "He that is spiritual judgeth all things, yet he himself is judged of

no man," (1 Cor. 2:15). He is the judge of all and yet none the judge of him.

(3) There are some impressions of the all sufficiency of God that is engraved on a Christian. So, "I have all and abound and am full," (Phil. 4:18). "As having nothing and yet possessing all things," (2 Cor. 6:10). So, "godliness with contentment is great gain," (1 Tim. 2:6). The Greek reads: *godliness with self-sufficiency is great gain.* So Solomon tells us that a good man shall be satisfied from himself, not from another but from himself. There is some kind of impression of the all sufficiency of God upon a Christian.

(4) There's a kind of omnipresence of God upon a Christian. Heaven and earth are the two great continents of all things. Now a divine soul is traveling in them both at once. "Our conversation is in heaven," (Phil. 3:12); though they themselves were on earth, yet their conversation was in heaven so that they are both in heaven and earth at once. Wherever God is, there the saints are, for they have their dwelling places in him. "Nevertheless I am continually with thee, thy right hand upholdeth me," (Psalm 73:23). A Christian runs through all states and things with God himself. He is led by his Father's hand through every state.

(5) There's a kind of immortality put upon a saint. Mortality is written on the face of all things that are below; everything is liable to the stroke of death. Yet a Christian,

though he dies daily, yet lives forever. Though the man dies, yet the saint does not; grace is never laid in the grave. "He that believeth in me shall never die," (John 11:26). That is, he shall never live uncomfortable, for an uncomfortable life is equivalent to death. And he that believes in me shall never die eternally; the second death has no power over him. He may die as a man, but he shall never die as a believing man.

(6) There's a kind of immutability and unchangeableness of a Christian. In regard to his state, he is immutable. He can never change, though in regard of the degrees of his state he is changing daily. He is a saint forever and he shall never lose the graces that he has received, for the gifts and callings of God are without repentance. That is, he never repents, nor exercises any acts of sorrow, for the bestowing of grace upon any of his people. A believer lives unchangeably in the midst of changes. He lives peaceably in the midst of troubles and cheerfully in the midst of wants. Thus you see that a saint has conformity and the resemblance of God on him.

2. The second position is that conformity is the ground of communion. The more likeness there is in any creature one to another, the more love; and the more love, the more desire of communion. Birds of a feather will flock together. Things that carry a contrariety can never admit of any community. What communion has light and darkness together, which are

opposite to each other? The light expels the darkness and the darkness draws a shadow over the light. The Holy Spirit tells us in plain language that light has fellowship with nothing but light, and darkness has fellowship with nothing but darkness. "If we say that we have fellowship with him and walk in darkness, we lie, and do not the truth: But if we walk in the light, as he is in the light, we have fellowship one with another and the blood of Jesus Christ his Son cleanseth us from all sin," (1 John 1:6-7). There can be no communion with Christ except there be a conformity to Christ. Now there are many souls that delude and deceive themselves and think they have none. But alas, if you are not made like Christ, you can never have communion with Christ in grace or communion with Christ in glory.

In this way you see this communion arises from the conformity that is in the saints to Christ. Likeness is the ground of love, and suitableness is the ground of intimacy. That is the reason why you say a man is known by his communion. Princes' tempers are judged by their favorites. The reason is because a man's spirit never closes in intimate society with any man, but one that has suitableness with himself. "There can be no communion between light and darkness, Christ and Belial," (1 Cor. 6:17). Where there is no conformity, there is no communion, (Rom. 8:29). What is the great end you aim at? To be like his Son. So then, when your conformity shall be perfect, then your communion shall be swallowed up in sight; for sight in heaven is but a perfect union.

CHAPTER 6: THE PROPERTIES OF COMMUNION

Second: to give you the properties of the communion. They are these six: It's (1) superlative and transcendent; (2) free and voluntary; (3) close and near; (4) growing and increasing; (5) spiritual and supernatural; and (6) delightful and complacent.

1. It's a superlative and a transcendent communion; a communion that is above all communions. It excels all other communions and fellowships in the inferior world. There are two very sad sights in the world; one is to see a bad man inflamed with joy and the other is to see a good man devoured and overwhelmed with sorrow. Let me pluck down the pride of the natural man and raise up the heart of the spiritual man.

There are many other communions in the world, but this is above them all: *The communion that the saints have with God compared with other communions.* It's as Saul, among the people, was higher by the head and shoulders than the rest of them. The sun, compared with the planets, is far larger and far more glorious than anyone of them—no, than all of them. You that take up the communion without God, below God, besides God, no (it may be in something) *against* God; know this that it is much inferior to the communion that the saints have with

God. "Let him kiss me with the kisses of his mouth: for thy love is better than wine," (Song of Solomon 1:2). It was the saying of a precious saint that *one hour's communion with God was worth more than the whole world.* And indeed the saints are able to set to their seal that this is true. You will see them doing of it, "For a day in thy courts is better than a thousand, I had rather be a doorkeeper in the house of God, than to dwell in the tents of wickedness," (Psalm 84:10). One day's communion with God is worth more than the entire communion you have in this world. You that are rocked in the cradle of creatures and take the cream of them that have all the bosoms of created excellences to receive from and to communicate yourselves also to, alas, there's more sweetness tasted in the enjoyment of the least part of God, than in the greatest part of the world. Are not waters much more pleasant in their springs than in their streams? The saints and people of God drink at the fountain's head when they go to God and take in all at the first hand. The creature's milk gives no sweetness but when God fills their breasts. The communion that the saints have with God is superlative and transcendent in a six-fold respect:

(1) The dignity and excellency of all communion are according to the persons with whom we communicate. "That which we have seen and heard, declare we unto you, that ye also may have fellowship with us," (1 John 1:3). Why? With whom is your fellowship? Our fellowship is with the Father

and with his Son Jesus Christ. The fellowship that the saints have is with all the persons in the Trinity. In this communion there are these two things: First, the persons dignify the communion, and second, the communion dignifies the persons that enjoy it. For a beggar to have communion with a king is a very high privilege, but nothing compared with the saints enjoying communion with God. Ordinary communion with extraordinary persons raises it to a great height.

(2) Our communion with God must be a superlative communion. Why? Because it is the foundation on which all other fellowships are laid. When we break with God, all creatures break with us. When man fell from his holiness, he fell from his happiness. When he fell from his image, he fell from his excellency. The creatures stood on the same terms with us as we stood with God and by falling from God, all creatures fell from us. There were two things that we lost in relation to the creatures: 1. Our dominion over them, and 2. Our communion with them. All men that live in their natural state have no real communion with the creature; all creatures are enemies to them since they themselves became enemies to God. Creatures had no longer their commission to be obedient to us than we were obedient to God. I observe now when once we are restored to God and brought into communion with heaven, all the creatures are restored to us when once we ourselves are brought to God. "I will betroth thee unto me

forever; I will hear the heavens, and the heavens shall hear the earth, and the earth shall hear the corn, and the wine, and the oil, and they shall hear Jezreel," (Hosea 2:19-22). There is a five-fold communion that is grounded on our communion with God. 1. The communion that the saints have with the angels is all grounded on the communion they have with Christ. 2. The communion that the saints of God have with one another. Saints should never have had communion with saints if they had not had communion with God. "These things write we unto you that ye also may have fellowship with us; and truly our fellowship is with the Father, and with his Son Jesus Christ," (1 John 1:3). 3. The communion of the church of the Jews with the Gentiles that's laid in their communion with God. 4. The communion the glorious saints have in heaven with the glorious saints on earth that's grounded on their communion with God, (Heb. 12:22-23). 5. The communion that we have with all creatures that's grounded upon our communion with Christ.

(3) This must be the most superlative communion that is made between God the Father and Jesus Christ and all the saints. Why? Because when once it begins, it never ends. Perpetuity adds an excellency to it. Things that are evil are much more evil by how much longer their continuance is. So it is in things that are good; they are much better by their continuance. There may be some interpositions of a saint's

communion at times, but no dissipation of it. The interruptions that the communion of the saints meets with are but as clouds before the sun that quickly make their departures again when it shines forth on them. Other communions often end as soon as they begin; they are lost as soon as they are found; they are taken out of our hands as soon as they are gotten into our hands. Friends quickly die and leave us behind them or it may be we ourselves die and leave our friends behind us, and so the knot of communion is untied. They are not long lived that have the longest life, but a saint in communion would never attain his end, if his communion should ever come to an end. Such as the building that's laid upon it, the foundation of all communion is laid in love, and love is laid from everlasting to everlasting. God must first cease to let out his affections to the saints before he can cease in communion with them.

(4) It must be the highest communion because it is the open door to all a saint's blessedness. So you have it in the text: I will meet them and bless them. What blessing did Jacob receive when the angel wrestled with him all the night? But Jacob's wrestling goes before his blessing. Our communion makes way for our blessedness. There are no favors but that which comes in through the gates of communion.

(5) It must be the highest communion because all other communions are but dark shadows and resemblances of it. The uttermost that all communions among all the creatures amount to is but a resemblance and a dark shadow of this communion with God. It's resembled by the vine and the branches, the head and members, a friend to a friend, the husband and the wife; but alas, these are but the fingers of the dial without to let us see how the wheels move therein. Look how much the substance outgoes the shadow, so much does the love of Christ, and our communion with him, outgo any resemblance that can be made of it.

(6) Our communion with God must be a superlative communion because all other communions are to be laid down in order to the taking up and keeping up of this communion with God. Look at the fellowship any man has or what communion he can have that is inconsistent with his communion with God and is to be laid down for the enjoyment of communion with God; therefore, it is the most transcendent communion.

I might give it to you in four more particulars: there is no communion as desirable, as profitable, as powerful, and as perfect as this communion with God. This is the first property of communion with God. It's a transcendent communion.

2. The second property of the saint's communion with God is that it's a free and voluntary communion. The

communion that the creatures have with God and that God has with them is not brought in by force. (1) On God's part to the creature, it's fee and voluntary. (2) On the creature's part to God, it's free and voluntary. God makes choice of the creature for communion with himself, for the unveiling of his glory, for the opening of his bosom, for the bestowing of his love, and for the pouring forth of his Spirit. God freely and voluntarily opens his bosom to the saints, and the saints do freely and voluntarily open their bosoms to God. "Behold, I stand at the door and knock; if any man hear my voice, and open the door, I will come in to him, and sup with, and he with me," (Rev. 3:20). The doors are not broken open, but they are set on when Christ comes in. Christ comes undeserved, and many times undesired, but where he does not find the will free, he makes the will free to embrace him. The will of God is in nothing more set forth to the creatures than in communion, and the will of the creature is in nothing more let out to God than in communion also. Communion is so much the more choice by how much the more it is chosen. "Draw me, and we will run after thee," (Song of Solomon 1:4). When Christ draws, she will not withdraw from him, but she will follow after him. The several dispensations of communion speak it out to be free communion.

(1) Some have a clearer and distinct communion with God than others have had. "And he said, if there be a prophet

among you, that I the Lord will make myself known to him in visions and dreams; But my servant Moses it is not so with him, for I will speak to him mouth to mouth (*not in dark speeches*) and the similitude of the Lord shall he behold," (Num. 12:6-8). Some men's communions are clearer and less clouded than others. Some men talk with God face to face, as men talk with their friends, but others see on the back parts of God; communion is more clouded to them. They cannot enter within the veils, but these are taken within all veils, and they have more naked views of divine glories than others have. Some souls have sweet enjoyments of communion with God, and yet do not have so clear discoveries as to be able to demonstrate their communion. But because communion is free and voluntary, and so God dispenses it according to the rules of his own will.

(2) Some men's communions with God are more constant than others; some walk continually in the light of his countenance and ever sit under the hearing of the joyful sound. Others complain again, as in, "O the hope of Israel, the Savior thereof in the time of trouble, why shouldst thou be as a stranger in the land, and as a wayfaring man that turneth aside to tarry for a night?" (Jer. 14:8). With some God stays but a little while; with others he takes up his dwelling. They are always under the dew droppings of divine communion and have the constant flowings in of a divine presence. He lies

down with some souls and rises up with them again. I have set God always before me says the prophet; he is at my right hand, I shall not fall. God was never out of his sight. His eye was fixed upon him and his soul was running out after him. "Nevertheless, I am continually with thee, thy right hand hath upheld me," (Psalm 73:23). It's a free and voluntary communion. Though desires are the actings of the affections, they are also the issuing forth of the will. "Awake O north wind, and come thou south, blow upon my garden that the spices thereof may blow out: let my beloved come into his garden and eat his pleasant fruits," (Song of Solomon 4:16). "I am by beloved's and his desire it towards me," (Song of Solomon 7:10). There is the going forth of desires to each other for the enjoyment of one another. No communion is as free as the communion that is between Christ and the saints, between God and his people.

3. The third property of the saint's communion with God is that it's a very close and near communion. So my test: I will meet them and bless them. Look as the union that is between Christ and a believer is very close and near, so the communion, that is between Christ and believers, is very close and near also. They are joined to one another. There are two things that hinder communion: (1) difference of persons and (2) distance of paces. Both of these are taken away in Christ when the soul comes to approach the presence of God and

stand before him. A soul cannot say as he said, "I shall see him, but not now, I shall behold him, but not nigh," (Num. 26:17). No, this communion is called an *appearing* before God. It is called a *drawing nigh* to God, a *supping* with God. It is not a communion at a distance, but a communion in presence. It is not a communion without doors, but a communion within doors. It is God's coming in to the soul, and the soul coming up more and more into God. "Let my beloved come into his garden and eat his pleasant fruits," (Song of Solomon 4:16). "I will come in to him and sup with him, and he with me," (Rev. 3:20). It is a soul creeping into the very bosom of Christ. It is as it were the child getting into his Father's arms, or the husband lying between the breasts of his spouse, (Song of Solomon 1:13). A bundle of myrrh is my well-beloved to me; he shall lie all night between my breasts, "Let us draw near," (Heb. 10:22). Observe all communion is according to the union. The further off anything is in union, the greater distance is the point of fellowship. So it is here, the nearer the union, the closer the communion. A child is further off in point of union then a spouse, a servant farther off than a child. The highest union has always the closest communion.

Jesus Christ and the saints have the nearest union, for they are made one Spirit. The bond of all union below is flesh, but the bond of all union above is Spirit. Jesus Christ and a saint is one, as the Father looks upon them all in him; he never looks on them as subtracted, but as united.

There is always the closest communion where there is the choicest love between Christ and the saints; therefore, the closest communion. Love cannot live at the least distance from its beloved. Love lets nothing come between or interpose between it and its object. It is like a falling mountain that breaks down all that is between it and its rest. Love is never so near, but it would still be nearer for when it sees its object in its eye, it would then have it *in his arms*.

4. The fourth property of the saint's communion with God is that it's a growing and increasing communion. Every day it creeps up to a greater height and to taller stature. No communion is capable of such increase as our communion with God. There are two things you may consider in relation to the souls of the saints: (1) they grow up by communion with God, and (2) they grow up in communion with God. The more a soul converses with God, and the more often it does approach to him, it comes to see a greater beauty in God, to taste a greater sweetness in God, and to enjoy a greater presences of God. Consider three *particulars:*

(1) look how a man's apprehension grows of God, so his communion grows with God. Most men's apprehensions are below God, but the best man's apprehensions are too low of God. When men raise apprehensions of God, and with

thoughts of the glory and excellency of God upon them, then they are raised in their communion with God. As the souls apprehensions of God are raised by degrees, so his communion with God is raised by degrees also, (Isa. 6:3). The angels have glorious acts of communion with God. They always behold the face of God; they are holy, holy, holy. When men have low understanding, slighting thoughts of the glorious majesty of God and of the holiness of God, they can never enjoy excellent and glorious communion with God. For such as a man's apprehensions are of God, such is his communion with God. There are three things that are according to our apprehensions of them: (i) Such as our apprehensions are, such will be our estimations. As we see things, so we prize them. (ii) Such will be our applications, if they are raised towards a thing; we apply ourselves to it that we may have the enjoyment of it. (iii) Such will be our communions; none shall ever take delight to draw near to those things where we see and judge no excellency.

(2) Consider as men grow up in conformity to God, so they will grow up in communion with God, for as conformity is a ground of communion, so the more conformity, the greater the communion still. As the life of holiness grows up within us so communion with God flows in on us. "That I may know him and the power of his resurrection," (Phil. 3:10). The more comfortable Paul was made to Christ's death, the more

communion he enjoyed in Christ's resurrection. "We beholding the same image as in a glass as the glory of the Lord are changed into the same image from glory to glory," (2 Cor. 3:18).

(3) The more a saint grows in largeness of affection, the more will he grow up in spirituality of communion; love draws the heart strongly after God. Many waters cannot quench love; neither can the clouds drown it. At the first entrance on our communion with God, the soul is but weak and poor. It has but some taste of God, but it comes for more until at last it feeds upon a full table. "If you have tasted that the Lord is gracious, (What then?), to whom coming as unto a living stone, disallowed indeed of men, but chosen of God, and very precious. Ye also as lively stones are built up a spiritual house," (1 Peter 2:3-4). The more we taste of the graciousness of God, the stiller do we come into communion with God.

It's very observable in the Song of Solomon that the spouse at first had but some kisses of the lips of Christ, but afterwards she is taken into his chambers, and at last she is brought into his banqueting house, into his house of wine. There are four things that communion leaves in the soul, after any precious acts that it has enjoyed.

(i) Communion leaves in the soul a sweet remembrance in it. "The king hath brought me into his chambers; we will be glad and rejoice in thee; we will remember thy love more than wine," (Song of Solomon 1:4). The acts of love of Christ showed to a soul in communion with him is increased by it. "When I remember these things, I pour out my soul in me," (Psalm 42:4). These things, what things? As the psalmist says, *When I went with the multitude that kept the holy day.* That is when I went with your saints to worship you, where I enjoyed communion with you.

(ii) It leaves an impression of grace and holiness of God upon the soul. "I rose up to my beloved, and my hands dropped with myrrh, and my fingers with sweet smelling myrrh upon the handles of the lock," (Song of Solomon 5:5). Moses' communion left an impression of the glory of God on him. When he comes from the mountain, he comes with his face shining. There are bright beams of God's face to be seen upon his face.

(iii) It leaves in a man a love to those ordinances— where he had communion. O! how much is the soul in love with those sermons in which communion with God is obtained and with those prayers in which he has the enjoyment of God.

(iv) It leaves in the soul an instinct after further fellowship and after further communion so that the whole desires of the soul are carried forth now after greater and larger enjoyments, after higher and more glorious incomes, and fresh influences of the divine presence. You never knew what it was to enjoy communion with God if your hearts do not run out after further and greater communion.

5. The fifth property of the saint's communion with God in ordinances is that it's spiritual and supernatural. First, it is not all the abilities of nature that can make up this communion. It is not all the education of the world that can bring a soul into the presence of God, or any parts and gifts that is able to raise the soul into communion with God. It is a spiritual communion; it is the Spirit of God coming down and taking the spirits of the saints up to itself. "I was in the Spirit on the Lord's day," (Rev. 1:10); when he was in the Spirit of the Lord, then he had communion with the Lord. "We all with open face behold as in a glass the glory of the Lord, are changed into the same image," (2 Cor. 3:18). We see the glory of the Lord, but what is the eye by which you see it? It is the Spirit of the Lord. This is an unerring rule that such as the union is such the communion must be. But the union that is spiritual, and therefore, the communion must be spiritual also. "They that are joined to the Lord are one spirit," (1 Cor. 6:17).

Second, such as the persons are enjoying communion, such is the communion of those persons. Now the persons enjoying communion are spiritual persons; therefore, the communion that they enjoy is spiritual. God is a Spirit and the saints are spiritual; and therefore, they have communion one with another in a spiritual manner.

Third, such as the means of communion is, such is the communion itself. Now all the means of communion are spiritual; therefore, the communion itself must be spiritual. The ordinances are all spiritual. They are not carnal ordinances though many persons use them carnally. Christ says the words are spirit and they are life. They are full of vigor, full of power, full of majesty, and full of authority. As no means attain their end, but such as are suitable to that end; so no end orders the means, but as such which agree with it. The communion the saints have with God is a spiritual communion; and therefore, look into your spirits, whether or not you do enjoy communion with God.

6. The sixth and last property of the saint's communion with God is that it is a delightful fellowship and communion. The soul comes to take up its delight and complacency in the enjoyment of God when once it is brought into communion with him, and God takes up his delight and complacency in the soul when once he comes to have communion with it. There is no communion as delightful as the communion that is made between God and the saints. There are many pathetical expressions (in Solomon's Song of Solomon) holding forth the inexpressible sweetness and delight in this communion between Christ and the soul, but two of them are chiefly remarkable and to be taken notice of. The words of the first text are these, "As the apple tree among

the trees of the wood, so is my beloved among the sons; I sat down under his shadow with great delight," (Song of Solomon 2:3). Or as it is in Hebrew, I delighted (myself) greatly (*chimmadti* being the conjugation piel, which intends and augments the signification of the root) and I sat down, or I desired exceedingly (for the proper and radical signification of the root *chamad* is he desired, and in piel *chimmed*, he desired greatly or exceedingly; and *chimmadti*, I desired greatly) and I sat down (to enjoy him and communion with him, and to taste the sweetness of his fruit. And what follows? His fruit was *matok lechikki*) sweet to my palate. Accordingly as I desired, which made me to delight myself abundantly in the enjoyment of him and communion with him. That is the force and emphasis of the first text. But further, as if this were not enough to express the sweetness and delightfulness of this communion; therefore, in the other text, Song of Solomon 5:16, has the same roots *chamad* and *matak* are raised up higher, as it were, to express a higher degree of delight and sweetness, (in this spiritual communion between Christ and the soul), so, his mouth is most sweet, *yes he is altogether lovely*. That is the expression in your translation. But the original words (which no translation in the world can reach nor rise to) are these: *Chicko mamtackkim vecullo machamaddim*; and word for word translated as: his mouth (*chic-co*) or the place of his mouth (is all) sweetness, full of (nothing but) sweetness; for the word *mamtakkim* is a noun in the plural number importing dulcetness sweetness. That is all sorts of sweetness, or sweetness itself, and all the species or kinds of sweetness are all laid up and hid as it were in the palate of his mouth to be tasted by souls taken up to communion and fellowship with him. That is the force of the first word *mamtakkim*, sweetness, from the former root *matak*, he was sweet. And the other word in this text, *vecullo machamaddim*, has the same and no less emphasis, importing this, and he is all, desires or delights, or all of him, all and every whit or part of him (*culla*) is nothing but delights (*machamaddim*, being also from the former root *chamad*, he desired, a noun in the plural number setting forth him and all the parts of him to be pleasures and delights that is most pleasant, most lovely and delightful; even to be all delights), and desires. That is most desirable and most worthy to be the object of all desires; and therefore, he is called *chemdat col haggojim*, "the desire of all nations," (Hag. 2:7). *Zeh dodi*, is my beloved, so sweet and so delightful, the tasting of his fruit in enjoyment of him, and communion with him. The believing soul says to invite all the daughters of Jerusalem to come and partake of such exceeding delight and sweetness, *betzillo*, under his shadows. For no shadow yields such shelter; no shadow yields such comfort. As the soul sitting under

Christ as a shadow that is enjoying her communion and fellowship with him. What delight does the tender Father take to have communion with his beloved child? And the loving husband takes to have communion with his beloved wife? What delight do friends take in having communion with each other? O! how much more and how much higher is the delights of Christ raised in having communion with the saints and the delights of the saints raised in enjoying communion with Christ. The spice of Christ to the Church is thus, "O my dove! That art in the clefts of the rocks in the secret places of the stairs, let me see thy countenance, let me hear thy voice, for sweet is thy voice, and thy countenance is comely," (Song of Solomon 2:14). So much for the properties of communion.

CHAPTER 7: THE ACTS OF COMMUNION

Thirdly, I come to the acts of communion. They are many and various. The chief of them are: mutual manifestation, mutual contemplation, mutual admiration, mutual delight and satisfaction, and mutual communication of secrecy.

The first act of communion is manifestations and that (1) of God to man and (2) of man to himself.

(1) Of God to man in three ways of his presence, of his glory, and of his grace:

(i) Of his presence says Jacob, "God is in this place," (Gen. 28:16). And "I will manifest myself to him," (John 14:21).

(ii) Of his glory, "To see thy power, and thy glory, so as I have seen thee in the sanctuary," (Psalm 63:3).

(iii) Of his grace, "Let us come boldly to the throne of grace," (Heb. 4:16). God in Gospel ordinances through Jesus Christ sits upon a throne of grace, and when we go to the throne of grace to receive from him, we must go with boldness. Now there are two chief acts that you are to exercise about this presence of God when it manifests itself to you in the use of ordinances.

1. The soul sees and observes this presence of God manifesting itself and beholds it. David says, "That I might

94

dwell in thy house to behold the beauty of the Lord, and to enquire in his temple," (Psalm 27:4). As the ordinances of God are the glory of a people, so the presence of God is the glory of the ordinances, and the soul that enjoys communion with God. It eyes and sees the glorious presence of God in ordinances.

2. There's not only an act of beholding, but there's an act of adoring the presence that we do behold, doing homage to it. The angels, that have a more immediate communion with God than we have, fall down before God and adore him. And so the prophet says, "Then said I, woe is me for I am undone because I am a man of unclean lips; for mine eyes have seen the King, the Lord of hosts," (Isa. 6:5). "And the twenty-four elders cast down their crowns at his feet and fall down before him," (Rev. 4:10).

(2) Secondly, there's an act of revelation of man to himself, to know himself. Man in himself is dark in discoveries of himself. "For God who commanded the light to shine out of darkness has shined in our hearts, to give the light of the knowledge of the glory of God, in the face of Jesus Christ," (2 Cor. 4:6). "The spirit of a man is the candle of the Lord, searching all the inward parts of the belly," (Prov. 20:27). It's not the presence of the Lord in heaven, but the presence of the Lord in ordinances that is the candle of the Lord. Now in this act of the revelation of the man to *himself*:

(i) It discovers the secrets of the heart. "And thus are the secrets of the heart made manifest," (1 Cor. 14:25).

(ii) It discovers the principles, grounds, and ends of his action. The word of God discovers it to him and the presence of God in it.

(iii) It passes a sentence on a man. "Son of man wilt thou judge them?" (Ezek. 20:3-4); that is, by ordinances. A soul is then judged by ordinances: First, when it is mightily ashamed in the divine presence for its non-conformity to God, and second, when it takes the judgment that the word gives and lies down with silence under it. This is the first act of communion, an act of manifestation of God to man and of man to himself; of God to man, of his presence, glory and grace; of man to himself, in the secrets of his heart and in the principles and grounds of his heart.

The second act of communion is mutual contemplation. The soul does continually converse with Christ by secret meditation and contemplation. There is a beholding of the beauty of Christ which is called the beauty of holiness. Holiness is the beauty of a saint and Christ is the beauty of holiness. The saints set forth Christ to be the fairest of ten thousands, fairer than the children of men; Christ replies again, *O thou fairest among women.* The saints behold and contemplate the beauty of Christ, and Christ beholds the beauty and contemplates the excellency of the saints. The saints are taken up with the love of Christ, and Christ is taken up with the love of them. In this way they admire the virtues of one another. You know it's never well with friends unless they are together. What a shift will lovers make to enjoy each other? So it is between the soul and the Lord. "When I awake, I am still with thee," (Psalm 139:18). Why? A man might have told David, God is in heaven and you are upon the earth. In my bodily presence I am from him, not with him but in the presence of Spirit and in the meditation and contemplation of the soul. I never lie down; I never rise up, but I am with you. By the Covenant of Grace and the ordinances of the Gospel you are to come to God, the Judge of all things. You have intimate fellowship with him, as well as, with the saints. Augustine says the soul does often and familiarly walk the streets of the New Jerusalem and seeing there the patriarchs, prophets, and the Lord Jesus Christ. This the soul does by fiducial reasoning and by high and glorious meditation and contemplation.

The third act of communion is mutual admiration. The soul is admiring those excellencies that are in God, and Christ is admiring those excellencies and being ravished with the beauties that are in them, "Thou has ravished my heart, my sister, my spouse," (Song of Solomon 4:9). In the book of Exodus it's said that the high priest carried the names of the children of Israel on his breastplate. A jewel set in the breastplate of Christ; O! how shining and glorious it is! The saints as jewels are very taking, but being set in Christ's breastplate is more taking. "This is my beloved, this is my friend, O you daughters of Jerusalem," (Song of Solomon 5:16).

The fourth act of communion between Christ and the soul does consist in mutual delight, satisfaction, contentment, and rejoicing in each other. There was great fellowship and communion between David and Jonathan, and they rejoiced in each other. There's great fellowship and communion between wife and husband. "Let her be as the loving hind to thee," (Prov. 5:19). "I will rejoice over thee, as a bridegroom rejoices over the bride," (Isa. 62:5). O! the contentment that the soul takes in Christ and the contentment Jesus Christ again takes in the soul that he has communion with it. "He shall see of the travail of his soul and shall be satisfied," (Isa. 53:11). "I shall be satisfied when I awake with thy likeness," (Psalm 17:15). *Chelek Jehovah guamma*; "The Lord's portion is his people," (Deut. 32:9). And so *chelki Jehovah merah naphshi*; "The Lord is my portion saith my soul," (Lam. 3:24). Therefore, the soul studies Christ and Christ studies the soul. The king shall take pleasure in your beauty. You know the command is to a man concerning his wife, "Let her breast satisfy thee at all times, and be thou ravished always with her soul," (Prov. 5:19). Now generally, the Lord Christ's people satisfy him because of his work in them at all times. It is the entire portion he looks for,

(Isa. 62:4). He calls her name *chephtzi bah*, or Hephzibah, my delight in her.

The fifth act of communion is communication of secrets. Love gives gifts and it gives counsels too. The carriage of a saint in communion when he receives the communion of secrets must be *in this way:*

1. He must come with holy and sanctified thoughts of God.

2. He must come with apprehensions and thoughts of his own vileness. To him will I look (says God) that is of a humble heart. With an eye of inspection? No, but with an eye of respect, with an eye of compassion, and with an eye of approbation.

3. He must come with seriousness of Spirit and with solidity of heart to the ordinances, if he would enjoy communion with God in them and have the secrets of God revealed to him.

4. All a man's graces should be acted when he comes to attend on God.

5. He must bring the Lord Jesus Christ in his arms. As we perform no service but by him so we have no communion with God but through him. Christ is a two-fold Mediator: First of reconciliation for enemies and strangers, and second, for communion and communication of secrets to those that are reconciled.

Now in all those and all other acts of spiritual communion there is one special and choice qualification of them that they are performed and acted with much intimacy or with very intimate and familiar correspondence between Christ and the soul which appears in these particulars:

1. The soul has a great deal of intimacy in those acts of communion with Christ. For it looks on him as reconciled as one that bears nothing but goodwill to it. It's ungodly men that look upon God as a stranger; God shows them the back and not the face, (Jer. 18:17), but it's not so with his people. He removes all clouds and shows them his face. He causes his face to shine upon them, "My meditations of him shall be sweet," (Psalm 104:37). What is that which sweetens David's meditation of the Lord? Truly the reason was because he looked upon God as reconciled and at peace with him; therefore, whatever was in God, was his. Not to look on God as a Judge, but as a Husband, as a Father reconciled. And so the soul has an interest in whatever is his. Thus God is said to be the rest of the soul, "Return to thy rest, O my soul," (Psalm 116:7). Consider your rest; for truly when the soul wanders from God, it is restless. That's an excellent expression. "My heart panteth," (Psalm 38:10); you read it, but in the original it is this, סְחַרְחַר לִבִּי *libbi secharchar*; my heart went about to and fro like a merchant. For it is from the root *sachar*, which signifies *to go about or to run hither and thither*, properly *to traffic*

and play the merchant in buying and selling. So the soul runs to this creature and is trading with that creature. But when once the soul sets on God, it rests there as upon a rock of ages.

2. Their fellowship with Christ is in things of the highest nature; therefore, there's a great deal of intimacy. A man may have acquaintance in ordinary things, but familiarity in things of the highest concernment. It argues a great deal of intimacy; your fellowship is in the Spirit. As the devil is an enemy to your fellowship with God in heavenly things and thing of eternity, (Eph. 6:12), so the intimacy you have with Jesus Christ is in things spiritual and of an eternal concernment, and they are these *four*:

(1) It's fellowship with Christ in his graces and the graces of his Spirit. "We have an unction from the holy one," (1 John 2:22).

(2) It's fellowship with Christ in the motions of his Spirit. They that have received the Spirit of Christ are led by that Spirit, (Rom. 8:14).

(3) It's fellowship with Christ in the sealings of his Spirit. "After you believed, you were sealed by the Spirit of promise," (Eph. 1:13).

(4) It's fellowship with Christ in the earnest of his Spirit, which I think is more than the sealing. Sealing puts the state out of controversy, but earnest gives a man a taste of that glory beforehand. As a wicked man in this life, by the spirit of

bondage, receives judgment, a kind of sense and taste of hell in his soul beforehand, (Heb. 10:27). So the Lord lets into the souls of his people a foretaste of glory. Here is a great deal of familiarity.

3. In the third place, this intimacy that the saints have with the Lord Jesus consists in this. They come to him with boldness and have access with boldness to the throne of grace.

It is called "drawing near," (Heb. 10:22). All ungodly men stand afar off from God. He comes to God as a stranger; he is afraid of him. But the drawing near of the children of God is called, "a lifting up their face to God," (Job 22:26). They shall have boldness in the presence of God, as a man that lifts up his face without fear in the presence of his intimate and familiar friend. "Their smell shall be as the wine of Lebanon," (Hos. 14:6-7). It is an observation of Galen: all other things grow old and will grow the worse for time; but wine, the longer you keep it, the better it will be; time does not make it grow worse. And that is the reason of that expression of our Savior: *He that has tasted of old wine does not by and by desire new.* Now they shall come into the presence of God and their services shall be accepted of him, as the wine of Lebanon. What is that? That is, (as one says), the older they are and the more often they come into the presence of God, the more acceptation they find with him because their smell is as the wine of Lebanon.

4. In the fourth and last place, they have a great deal of intimacy which appears in this—they are always calling one another to further fellowship and are never satisfied. Our Savior Christ is always crying, "Open to me my love, my sister, and my spouse," (Song of Solomon 5:2). And the church is always calling, "The Spirit saith come, and the bride saith come," (Rev. 22:17); "come away my beloved, come away like a roe or a young hart upon the mountain of spices," (Song of Solomon 8:14). By these mountains of spices, I conceive to be meant *the promises*. And the Lord's making this on them is for their accomplishment. "Set me as a seal upon thine heart," (Song of Solomon 8:6). All this is nothing else but the church still calling to the Lord for further fellowship. True grace is a spark begun here, and it will never cease aspiring until it has gotten to Christ, who is the fountain of all in glory.

CHAPTER 8: THE END OF COMMUNION

Fourthly, I come to the end of communion; why God will have any fellowship at all with the saints; and seeing he will have fellowship and communion with them, why he does not immediately translate them to glory.

Observe—he that accomplishes the best and the greatest ends is the wisest man. The more ends any action accomplishes, the more excellent is that action. Mordecai's action was a most excellent one because it brought about so many ends. There was a great plot defeated, great enemies subdued, the state of the Church restored, the king's affections rectified, and his honor and advancement. There are eleven ends why God will have fellowship and communion with his people.

1. The first great end of God in communion is that he might manifest and impart himself to the creature. God's imparting of himself to the creature is an act of communion and the very end of communion too. "I will come to him and manifest myself to him," (John 14:21). There were two ends for which God created the angels: The one for glory and the other for communion that they might behold his face and that he might impart himself to them. There is a double end of communion. Some have communion for need; others have it

for delight. Some have communion for need; they impart their wants to have them supplied. Others have communion for delight; their communion is out of abundance of desire for communication. Not that they might receive from others, but that they might give to others. God does not have communion with all creatures out of need, but out of delight, not that he needs the creature, but that he might give forth of his abundance to the creature. God sets apart the man that is godly for himself; not for service only, but for communion and communication also. This is one of the great ends of God in communion that he might impart and communicate himself to the creature.

2. The end why God will have communion with the saints is that he might thereby set forth to the saints the perfection of the mediation of Christ and that is these two things: (1) In his being able to cure all the wounds and bruises that sin had made upon a man. By sin we lost both our image and our fellowship. Now Jesus Christ does not only make peace with God so that he does not destroy us, but also raises a way of communion with God to receive us. That's a type of Christ. "I will meet with thee, and I will commune with thee from above the mercy seat," (Exod. 25:22). (2) He is able to give you more perfect communion than Adam had, as he gives you a more perfect righteousness. As we do not have a distinct righteousness from Christ's righteousness, so we do not have

a distinct fellowship from Christ's fellowship. All the communion that Christ has in the human nature with the Father is for us and in our behalf.

3. The third end of why God will have fellowship and communion with us is that in this fellowship all other fellowships may have their foundations laid. There had never been any kind of fellowship if there had not been first this kind of fellowship. When you break with God, all creatures break with you, for on the same terms that we stood with God did all creatures stand with us. The devils have no fellowship among themselves. Other creatures that are separated from God have no fellowship at all. But now the saints of Jesus Christ have fellowship with the angels. I, with all the saints, shall sit down with Abraham, Isaac, and Jacob in the kingdom of heaven. They have fellowship with the angels. Jacob's ladder, which is Jesus Christ, is where the angels come down and go up again; and they have fellowship with the saints. The communion between saints and saints is grounded on the communion that is between Christ and the saints. "That in the dispensation of the fullness of time, he might gather together in one all things in Christ, both which are in heaven, and which are on earth, given to him," (Eph. 1:10).

4. The fourth end of why God will have communion with his saints is that he might confirm them and make them like himself. God loves to see his own picture upon his own

people. The more any man is molded into the sorry things of the world, the more like them he is, the more communion he has with them, the more conformity. "He that walks with the wise shall be wise," (Prov. 13:20); so it is with the saints. The communion they have with God, the more conformity they have to him, for communion makes conformity and carries it on to a greater height. What is the reason the angels are more holy than men? It is because they have more communion with God than men have. What is the reason the glorified saints are more holy than the gracious saints are? It's because they have more communion with God. What's the reason one saint is more holy than another? It's because he has more communion with God than the other. According to the degree of our communion, such will be the degree of our holiness and conformity to God.

5. The fifth end of God's communion with the saints is that he may act and strengthen their graces. "While the king sitteth at his table, my spikenard sendeth forth the smell thereof," (Song of Solomon 1:12). Everything that comes nearer to its center moves swifter. Communion with God and the soul's enjoyment of God is the very center of it. And the nearer it comes to this, the swifter still it moves. It is observable of Abraham when he put forth the greatest act of humility in his communion with God, "O Lord I am but dust and ashes," (Gen. 18:27). And Jacob put forth the highest act of zeal in

communion with God, "I will not let thee go except thou bless me," (Gen. 32:26). And Moses put forth the greatest act of prayer in his communion with God, "O! Lord, pardon the sin of this people which is very great," (Exod. 34:9). One of the great ends that God aims at in communion is the exercise of your graces. He would not have the graces of his people to lie still, to be like swords rusting in the scabbards, but he would have them exercised. He would have your patience set at work in waiting upon him, your faith set at work in resting on him, your zeal set a work in longing after him, and your zeal set at work in acting for him. God does not love any heavenly talent that is wrapped up in a napkin. He was a sinful servant that was a slothful servant who laid up his master's talent when he should have laid out his master's talent. God loves to see us exercise all our graces and it is then that he has communion with us.

6. The sixth end of why God will have communion with the saints is that he may sweeten the whole course of our lives. While we are in this world we meet with many bitter things, and it's only communion with God that can put sweetness into them. Jesus Christ was a man of sorrows, and what upheld his life? Only communion with God, "The Lord stood by me and strengthened me," (2 Tim. 4:17). Now that which upheld the life of Christ is that which upholds the life of every Christian, and that is communion with God. Paul

makes use of the same words, "The Lord stood by me, and strengthened me, whose I am, and whom I serve," (2 Tim. 4:17). This is the mighty end that God aims at in communion that he may sweeten all the course of the pilgrimage while we are going to heaven. This is the bunch of grapes that God gives his people to feed upon in their wilderness state. They would be out of heart if they had no communion with him. This is that sweet wood that is cast into the waters at Marah to make them sweet and pleasant.

7. Therefore, God has communion with his people that he may prepare their hearts for desertions. That they may be affected with them when they come, and that they may not be dejected under them though they long continue that they may not think their cloud shall never be blown over, though their sun is hidden.

(1) That they may be affected with desertions. David says, "Thou didst hide thy face, and I was troubled," (Psalm 30:7). If he had never seen the face of God, he would never have been troubled for God's hiding of his face. The saints of God, if they had not some tastes of communion with him, wound never be troubled by his withdrawal from them.

(2) That they may not be dejected under them. David calls to mind his song that he made in the night and the remembrance of that was exceedingly sweet and exceedingly pleasant to him. The remembrance of former communions

that he had with God bore up his spirit when many troubles were upon him.

8. The eighth end of why God will have communion with his people is to put them out of taste with all the pleasures of sin and the creature. "And the peace of God which passeth all understanding, keep your hearts and minds," (Phil. 4:7). It's usually when any *epitaph* of God is added to a thing that it signifies and notes the excellency of it. It's the peace of God; a peace that comes from God; a peace that brings to God; a peace that makes us live like God in such sweetness, peace, and contentment. Now this peace puts a man's mouth out of taste of any of the sweetness and of the pleasures of sin. David says, "Thy loving kindness is better than life," (Psalm 63:3). The church says, "And let him kiss me with the kisses of his mouth, for thy love is better than wine," (Song of Solomon 1:2). There is nothing that puts us out of taste with the pleasures of sin so much as a soul's tasting of communion with God. When a soul has drunk the old wine, it does not care for drinking of the new because the old was better. The loving kindness of God in communion with him is that which takes off the palate from tasting sweetness anywhere else. The more any soul is brought into communion with God, the less it desires the pleasures of sin.

9. The ninth end of what God aims at in giving the soul communion with himself is that it might aggravate their sins

in the day of repentance. Sins against communion are great aggravations. Solomon departed from the Lord when he had appeared to him twice which mightily aggravated his sin, (1 Kings 11:9). God kept an exact account of his manifestations that he might aggravate Solomon's sins in the day of his repentance. O! when a soul comes to sit down and consider, I have not only sinned against so many mercies of God and so long tired out the patience of God, but I have sinned against communion with God. Jesus Christ took into his, "banqueting house, and his banner over me was love; He stayed me with flagons, he comforted me with apples, his left hand was under my head, and his right hand did embrace me," (Song of Solomon 2:4-6). And yet I sinned myself out of the sweet embraces of Christ. O! how does this melt the heart when it comes to mourn for sin. The sense of the sweetness of his communion that he had with God puts double tears into his eyes and double sighs into his spirit. There's no such aggravation of sin as communion with God.

10. God has communion and fellowship with his people; therefore, he meets them that he might bless them, (Exod. 20:24). Communion times are times when all requests are granted. King Ahasuerus grants the request of Esther when he comes to sit with her at a banquet of wine. The greatest blessing that ever the saints do enjoy is in times of communion with God. O! then, how their consciences are

filled with peace! O! how are their hearts filled with joy! God makes large distributions of spiritual blessings when he admits the soul into communion with himself. What blessing is there that the soul may not have when it has communion with God in ordinances?

11. The eleventh end of God's communion with his people is that his fellowship here may be the first fruits of glory hereafter. When God will bestow any great mercy on a man, he gives him a taste of it beforehand that he may set him upon more earnest and eager longings after it. God's people have the first fruits of all their mercies in this world and the full crop of them all in another world. When the soul is made to taste of the sweetness of communion with God, O! how it longs to be with God. How many prayers does the soul make to God that he would take it home to himself that it might lie in his arms and dwell in his presence! "I desire to be dissolved and to be with Christ, which is best of all," (Phil. 1:23). What was the ground that raised up such desires in Paul to be with Christ? It was because here he had tasted the sweetness of Christ. And if Christ in this world was so sweet, if Christ on earth was so sweet, then Christ in heaven would be much sweeter. And on this ground the church calls to Christ, "Make haste my beloved, and be thou like a roe or young hart upon the mountain of spices," (Song of Solomon 8:14). When Christ had told the church that he would return again to her to have

more communion with her, she cries out, "Amen, even so come Lord Jesus," (Rev. 22:20). She puts her prayers to Christ's promises and says, "Amen Lord, let it be so."

CHAPTER 9: USES OF THE DOCTRINE

Application: There are three uses I shall make of this point: 1. information, 2. examination, and 3. exhortation.

1. For information: Is it so that the main end of God in the establishing and setting up of ordinances is communion for himself? Here I draw these six *inferences:*

(1) Behold here the infinite delight that God takes in the society of all his saints that he would set up all ordinances for this end to have communion with them that he might have communion with him, that he might have the enjoyment of them, and that they might come to the participation of him. It's a wonder of mercy and of condescension that the most High should stoop to such low persons. He that had infinite blessedness in the society and in the enjoyment of himself and took so great a delight in his Son and in the society of the angels that he should take any delight to impart himself to poor sinful dust and ashes, to men, no to worms and not men.

When men set up a variety of means for the accomplishment of their ends, it's a great sign that their hearts are very much set upon them. Consider what variety of ordinances God has set up for the communication of himself to believers.

(2) Behold here, what should be the main end of the saints, in the use of all ordinances, namely, communion and fellowship with God. Look what was God's end in using of ordinances—in praying we should seek the face of God and in hearing we should hear the voice of God. Hear what God the Lord will say; and in meditating, my meditation of thee shall be sweet; and in conference, "They should talk of the glory of thy kingdoms and speak of all thy power," (Psalm 145:11). In receiving the Lord's Supper, what should be a saint's greatest delight in coming to the spiritual banquet? It should be meeting with Christ in that ordinance. We oftentimes lose all the blessings of the means because we do not propound to ourselves communion with God as the end. Many souls that come to sermons, Christ may say to them as he said to those, "What went ye out into the wilderness to see? A reed shaken with the wind?" (Matt. 11:7). You are to do as the wise virgins did, to go forth and meet the bridegroom and to trim your lamps for the meeting of him. If communion is not your end in ordinances, nothing will be available to you in ordinances. You will lose all the ordinances that you enjoy unless you meet with Christ in them.

(3) Is communion with God the great end of God in ordinances? Here then learn this that when communion with God in ordinances is not enjoyed, then the ultimate end of all the ordinances is frustrated. You lose the end for which all

preaching, praying, and hearing was ordained. While communion is missed and while you have no ordinances with God, ordinances never attain their appointed ends. How sad is it to use the means and never attain the end, and yet this is the case of thousands of souls that live under choice administrations, and yet are never brought into a state of communion. They are so far from enjoying communion with God that they do not know what it is to have communion with God though it be declared to them. How many are there that lie a long time at the pool, and yet never see any angel come down to sir the water; that lie by the sides of the pool, but are never put into the pool? O! how said it is that such excellent ordinances should lose their ends and that we should so long have the enjoyment of them, and yet never be bettered by them. That we should never attain those ends for which they were ordained.

(4) Is it so that the main end of God in establishing and setting up of ordinances is to enjoy communion with himself? Then let every soul take heed of throwing down of ordinances. Let every soul be exceedingly tender of the appointments of God. If they throw away the means of their communion with God, and live without God in the world, then they are not tied to God in his ordinances. And in my own experience, I have known many men grow worse, but never any man grow better by neglecting ordinances. There is

no communion to be had with God but in ordinances; and therefore, if you go from ordinances you will be fetched home by *a rod*, if you belong to God. Whatever you do, be very tender of Gospel ordinances. "For if he that despised Moses, his law died without mercy under two or three witnesses; of how much for punishment shall they be thought worthy, that trample under foot the blood of the covenant, wherewith they were sanctified and count it an unholy thing?" (Heb. 10:28). O! it's sad to see now how many souls there are that cast dirt on those ordinances that are the chariots in which Jesus Christ rides to take up souls into communion with himself.

(5) If communion is the main end of God in setting up of ordinances, behold then when it is and why it is that the saints of God are so much troubled when they lack the sensible enjoyment of communion with God. They know the truth of this truth; the ordinance in its end is lost to them. When a child goes out to seek his father and cannot find him, it's a great grief to him. Believers go out in Gospel ordinances to seek after God, and when they cannot find him, it must be very grievous to their spirits, "by night upon my bed I sought him whom my soul loved, but I found him not," (Song of Solomon 3:1). Divine endeavors do not always meet with divine success. She sought him, but she did not find him. So many a soul comes to meet with God in an ordinance, but God is withdrawn from them. They cannot see his face though they

come to seek his face. The sorest affliction that a child of God lies under or can lie under in this world is the withdrawal of God from ordinances; when he thinks to find God in them, he is departed from them. They shall go with their flocks and their herds to seek after the Lord, but they shall not find him, for he has withdrawn himself.

(6) Is it the main end of God in setting up ordinances that his saints might have communion with him? Then learn here the ground why the saints set so high a price upon and are so often found in divine ordinances. It's because they meet there for communion with God. Now the meetings with God are the grounds of their appearing before him. Alas, it's not their meeting together that they aim at, but their meeting with God that they look after, if God is wanting, all is wanting; if God is there, nothing is wanting. Ordinances alas can do nothing without God. They are but painted swords in dead men's hands. They cannot raise the heart when it is fallen. They cannot refresh the heart when it is sad. They cannot enlighten the soul when there is a cloud on it. They cannot draw the heart to heaven when it is earthly. They cannot resolve any doubts that are upon their spirits. Alas, if there were nothing but the very ordinances, believers would never be so often in the use of them. If there were nothing but a little bread and wine at a sacrament, who would sit down at it with such great delight? If there were nothing but praying

in prayer, who would lose any time about it? If there were nothing but hearing in hearing, if there was not the power of God going along with the voice of man, what is it? And therefore, when you see the saints and people of God so often employing themselves about spiritual ordinances, when you see them begin the day with prayer and end the day with thanksgivings, and when you see them fixing their souls to meditate on God, you may well conclude there is more than the bare ordinance. No, in every ordinance remember it's not for the ordinance's sake, but for communion with God which was the main end why God set up ordinances.

2. For examination: How you may know whether you have had any fellowship and communion with God or not.

This is a serious question and deserves more than a slight answer. Communion with God is a thing of more concernment and of greater moment than most men are aware of, and we are used to trying things that will not be taken from us without trial. Consider three *things*:

(1) God has scales to weigh all your graces.

(2) He has touchstones to try all your graces.

(3) He has winnowing fans to sift all your graces.

"Thou hast a name to live and art dead," (Rev. 3:2); and then you used to try those things where there may be credit. Sometimes men think they have fellowship with God in ordinances when they do not, and sometimes men deny fellowship with God in ordinances.

That is, first, some men think they have fellowship with God in ordinances when they do not. There are two things that look like fellowship and communion with God in ordinances that are not.

(1) There are some imperfect approaches of God to the souls of unregenerate men in ordinances when there are no reciprocal approaches of the spirits of unregenerate men to God.

(2) When their spirits are only passive and not active, God calls upon them to seek his face, but their hearts never answer. "Lord thy face will I see," (Prov. 27:8), as the heart of the righteous do.

Secondly, some men deny fellowship with God in ordinances, which is common. Take these two *distinctions:*

(1) First distinction: Communion with God in ordinances is sometimes secret and sometimes more manifest. First, it is secret. God does not always speak peace with a loud voice. He sometimes speaks peace with a still voice. There communion with God is more secret, "My beloved put in his hand by the hole of the door, and my bowels were moved for him. I rose up to open to my beloved and my hands dropped with myrrh and my fingers with sweet smelling myrrh upon the handles of the locks," (Song of Solomon 5:4-

5). Secondly, it is more manifest. Sometimes they are in hidden rooms, in secret chambers together. At other times they are walking in the open galleries.

(2) Second distinction: There's a sanctifying communion, and there's a ravishing communion. The sanctifying communion may be where the ravishing communion may not be, "make me to hear joy and gladness," (Psalm 51:8). David had a sanctifying communion before, but now he begs for a ravishing communion with God that would raise him up to a rejoicing in God.

Now you may know whether you have fellowship with God in ordinances or not by three things: by something before duty, in duty, and after duty.

First, by something before duty. If you have communion with God, you may know it by these three characters.

(1) If God raises up your heart to make fellowship your end in duty. "O! show us the father and it sufficeth us," (John 14:8), that was the disciple's end in their prayer to Jesus Christ. Show us the Father; nothing but the Father would suffice them. So when you come to ordinances and say, "O! that I might see the going of God my King in his sanctuary!" God will never deceive the expectations of his people. These expectations are raised by him, and they shall be fulfilled by him. "I know the thoughts that I think towards you, saith the

Lord, thoughts of peace, and not of evil, to give you an expected end," (Jer. 29:11). They looked for peace; God says an olive branch shall be sent them. They expect my presence; they shall find my presence. If God beforehand raises up your heart to make fellowship your end in all your actions, then you may certainly conclude you shall have fellowship with him.

(2) If God beforehand put your heart into a suitable frame to the duty, then you may assure your soul. You shall have fellowship with God in the duty. If you find those graces exercised by you, the duty calls forth from you. When God called Moses into the mount, he was sure to have communion with God. Why? Because God gave him such dispositions, as fitted him for communion. When once the heart is put into a communion frame, it shall never go without it. If your shoes are put off and the place on which you stand is holy ground, never fear, but you shall enjoy communion with the holy God. There is a remarkable passage the psalmist has, (Psalm 10:17); expressly pointing at this that God does first put the spirits of his people in a frame, suitable to communion with himself. And secondly, he comes to them with a blessing, inclining his ear to hear and accept them favorably or that whenever the Lord does put the hearts of his people to a prepared frame, then he does incline his ear and hear them. The words are those *tachin libam* (there is the first) you will fit, dispose,

direct, or prepare their heart; or you will cause their heart to prepare itself, as it were. For *tachin* is the future hiph from the root *chun*, he prepared or fitted and then observe what follows. When once you have thus fitted and prepared their heart, then *takshib oznckah*, you will prepare your ear to hear; or you will cause your ear to be heard and to be attentive in hearing their suits and supplications. For the word *takshib* is also future hiph from the root *kashabiknal*, he was attentive or he heard with attention. So that God never puts his people into a prepared posture for communion, but he *gives* them communion; when duties answer to our hearts, and our hearts answer to our duties. This is the workmanship of God, to frame the heart for duty, as well as cut out duty for the heart.

And therefore the psalmist knowing this that it is the order and work of God: First to prepare the heart for communion and then to incline his own ear to hear his people and to entertain communion with them in ordinances. He does observe this order and follows it with a practice suitable to it in his daily addresses to God that is so: wherever he does find his heart put into a fitted and prepared frame for communion with God, he does not let it die again and go out of frame by a slothful neglect of such a disposition of heart. No, but he immediately sets himself to duty, to worship God, and to the acts of his worship, in his ordinances, as he expresses himself in another psalm. Psalm 57:7, thus, *nachon libbi elohim, nachon libbi*, (there is the first; he finds his heart fitted and prepared for communion with God). My heart (says he) is fitted or prepared (for the word *nachon* is the passive conjugation niphal signifying *he is fitted or prepared*, from the same root in the former text *chan*, he *fitted or prepared* in the active. And so it is rather to be rendered, *prepared*, or *fitted*, then *fixed*, so, *libbi*, my heart, *nachon*, is *fitted or prepared*). O! God, my heart is fitted or prepared (for communion with you). Well, what follows? He presently sets himself on that great duty and ordinance of communion with God in the praising of his name and singing forth those praises, as in the words immediately following in the same verse thus, "My heart is prepared, O! God, my heart is prepared," (Psalm 57:7); therefore, *ashidah va-azameral*, "I will sing and give praise," (Psalm 57:7).

(3) When the heart is carried forth in its utmost strength after duty, then you shall enjoy communion with God. Daniel sets his face towards Jerusalem, and the text says that, "at the beginning the angel of the Lord came and touched him: O! Daniel, greatly beloved of the Lord, thy prayer is heard," (Dan. 9:23). When the soul puts forth his greatest strength in duty, then it enjoys communion with God most in that duty. The more active you are in employing yourself

124

about this work, the more incomes from God will there be in this work. That's the first particular.

Secondly, in the duty. If there are ravishing discoveries, the heart knows it. God is his own witness in the Spirit. But if there is but a humbling fellowship, though there is not ravishing discoveries, it's an evidence. Now the dispositions of the soul in the duty which speaks communion with God are *these:*

(1) It is a very humble fellowship. It lays a man very low in his own eyes and raises God very high. How ready are we then to cry with Peter, "Lord depart from me, I am a sinful man," (Luke 5:8). The heart will be humble and the presence of God will be dreadful.

(2) The appearance of grace will be powerful. It will set the heart against every sin. When Moses came from the mount of communion, how zealous was he against the sin of idolatry?

(3) There will be an answering of the heart, for it is an echoing fellowship. The Lord says, you are my people, and they will say, you are my God. If he says, *seek you my face,* they will answer, *your face Lord will I seek.*

(4) It will be a heating fellowship. The disciples said, "Did not our hearts burn within us, while he talked with us?" (Luke 24:32). O! it will be a heating fellowship. It will kindle

fresh flames of love towards Jesus Christ. It will make your souls burn towards heaven.

Thirdly, after the duty, you may know whether you have fellowship by these *particulars:*

(1) It will leave a sweet remembrance behind it. "When I remembered these things, I poured out my soul in me; for I had gone with the multitude, I went with them to the house of God, with the voice of joy and praise, with a multitude that kept holy day," (Psalm 42:4). The soul can never forget those times of communion that it had with God, nor those bosom embraces, nor those sweet kisses that it had from the lips of Christ. These mercies are too great to be forgotten by a soul that does enjoy communion with God.

(2) It leaves an instinct in the soul after further fellowship with God. If a man falls into sin but once, it leaves proneness in a man to fall into it again. So it is in communion with God, if a many enjoys communion with God but once, it leaves a greater proneness and aptitude in the man to look after communion with God again. A soul that has had communion and fellowship with Christ, O! how does it long after further fellowship with him.

(3) It leaves in a man love to those ordinances in which it had communion with God. O! how is the soul in love with those prayers which brought Christ to it and in love with that word in which Jesus Christ spoke to his soul. How is it taken

with every ordinance, wherein the influences of heaven are distilled and dropped on them?

(4) It leaves an impression on the soul of the holiness of God. The holiness of God is of a transforming nature. "They took knowledge of them that they had been with Jesus," (Acts 4:15). They saw that they had enjoyed communion with God. Why? There were such beams of the majesty and the beauty and the glory of God left upon them, that they that saw them might easily know that they had seen God and had enjoyed communion with him. And it's said of Stephen, they beheld his face as the face of an angel when he was before council.

(5) If you have fellowship and communion with God, you will have acquaintance with God and familiarity with him. "Acquaint thyself with God," (Job 22:21). A soul cannot enjoy communion with a stranger until he is familiarized to his acquaintance. Communion speaks the choicest familiarity between persons. If your souls have had communion and fellowship with God, then you are brought into acquaintance with God.

(6) If your souls have enjoyed communion and fellowship with God, you will be sure to keep God company and walk with God; let others walk which way they please. It is said of Enoch, to his praise that he, "walked with God (Gen. 5:24). And God spoke to Abraham, "walk before me and be thou perfect," (Gen. 17:1).

(7) A soul that has communion and fellowship with God in ordinances is sensible of all. God withdrawals—he knows when God comes in and when God goes out at an ordinance. How many people are there that never mind, either the accesses or recesses of Christ or the Spirit when they come in to appear before God in ordinances.

(8) There will be a sweet agreement between Christ and the soul. Can two walk together except they be agreed in what path they shall go and what steps they shall take? That which was God's way shall be the soul's way. God will not go one way and let the soul go another, because then it can have no communion; but when God and the soul tread both in the same steps, there are sweet agreement and delightful harmony between them.

(9) A soul that has communion with God highly prizes the presence of God and the presence of the Lord Jesus Christ. Moses says, "If thy presence goes not along with us; carry us not from hence," (Exod. 33:15). And nothing gives the soul contentment if it has lost communion until it is restored again. It can bear anything better than a breach in its communion. No loads lie as heavy on it as a departed Savior. How does the soul lament after the Lord when it cannot find the Lord? It is restless until it comes to lie in its beloved's bosom.

Lastly, a soul that has fellowship and communion with God cuts off all other contrary fellowship that is inconsistent with it. It cuts off all sinful and carnal fellowship. They will have no fellowship with the unfruitful works of darkness that have fellowship and communion with the Father of lights.

CHAPTER 10: EXHORTATION

3. For exhortation to press you to look after communion with God. There are three things that we are to look after to attain to communion with God: We must have a right path, we must have a staff of strength and power, and we must have true ascents and fellowship.

First, we must have a right path, and that path is Jesus Christ. There is no coming to the Father but by the Son, "I am the way," (John 14:6). There is a choice way to God, but there is no choice of ways to come to God. Pass by one you pass by all, "For the Law made nothing perfect, but the bringing in of a better hope did; by which we draw nigh unto God," (Heb. 7:19). What is the better hope? It is Jesus Christ; hope depends so much on him for the best things that he is called *our better hope*, by which with assurance we may draw nigh to God. That's the apostle's encouragement, "By the blood of Jesus we have boldness to enter into the holiest," (Heb. 10:19).

Secondly, we must have a staff of strength and power, and that's the Spirit of God—"praying in the Holy Ghost," (Jude 20). As it's the office of Christ to intercede with God for us, so it's the office of the Spirit to intercede in us. The prayers that go up to God, come down from God.

There are two burdens that are too heavy for us to bear: First, the burden of sins, and second, the burden of suits.

Thirdly, we must have true ascents and footsteps; else we shall never come up to communion with God.

There are six ascents and footsteps by which we ascend to the throne of God for the enjoyment of communion with him.

(1) The sense of self-indignation: We never enjoy communion with the fullness of God until we see the emptiness that is in ourselves. A full soul loathes the honeycomb, though it has never so much sweetness in it; the whole never prizes the physician's medicines. A sense of want draws the creature down to earth and then leads it up to heaven.

(2) The sense of our own utter inability to supply our own necessities. "Whom have I in heaven but thee? And there is none upon earth that I desire besides thee; my flesh and my heart faileth, but God is the strength of my heart, and my portion forever," (Psalm 73:25-26). If there is anything that you expect satisfaction from besides God, you will never come to communion with him. You will then look after fellowship with him when you see all your happiness in him.

(3) The footstep to communion with God is a sense of our own unworthiness that God should give supplies to us. When Jacob was brought so nigh to fellowship and communion with God when he was struggling with God and would not let him go until he had got a blessing, then he let go

all opinion of worth in himself to receive a blessing, "I am not worthy of the least of all thy mercies," (Gen. 32:10). There is no drawing near to the most high God without low thoughts of ourselves. The proud look disdainfully on God and meet with disdain from him.

(4) The footstep to communion is the clear knowledge and full acknowledgement of the power of sufficiency of God to help us and to fill us, (Heb. 11:6). He that comes to God must believe that God is and that he is a rewarder of them that diligently seek him. What's that? It lies in two things: First, that God needs no creature, and second, that he is enough to supply the needs of every creature.

(5) The footstep to communion is to believe that the Lord stands ready to embrace us in all our comings to him and to give us all the good that we come for. To believe that he is ready to supply us in every good we seek from him. We honor God most when we expect the greatest incomes of mercy from him. "He hath not said to the seed of Jacob, seek ye me, (*tohu*), for a vain, void, and empty nothing," (Isa. 45:19). The greatness of God gives him power and his goodness gives him will to supply us; therefore, we should believe without doubting his readiness to supply us. "Let us draw near in full assurance," (Heb. 10:22). In what assurance must we come? Even in this that we shall be answered in whatever we ask. As faith must be mingled with every word of precept that God

speaks to us, so it must be mingled with every word of prayer that we speak to him. "If any lack wisdom, let them ask it of God that giveth to all men liberally and upbraideth not," (James 1:5-6).

(6) The footstep of our communion with God is boldness in all our approaches to him. As God opens his heart freely, so we must open our mouths boldly. Holy boldness is the highest act of faith and the nearest step to God. When the soul has got this high, it is upon the top of Jacob's ladder, "Let us come boldly to the throne grace," (Heb. 4:16). Boldness is a grace that is most suitable to the throne of grace. Let one speak with reverence. We have gone to God's side when we come with boldness; grace can step no higher. The next degree of ascent is to be swallowed up in glory. In every ordinance we have a vision of God by faith, and in every duty, we should come to God with boldness and joy.

CHAPTER 11: CONCLUSION

To conclude all: Would you have communion with God in ordinances? Then let me commend to you these five things.

First, there must be a being near to God before there can be a drawing near to God. You must labor after reconciliation before you can enjoy communion. While you are enemies you will be strangers. Until God is brought near to you, you can never draw near to God. We are first brought near to God by the blood of Christ before we have communion with God in ordinances.

Secondly, he that desires communion with God in ordinances must look on God as present and not as absent from him, without this, we can never enjoy communion with him. There's a, "high throne," (Rev. 4:6), which is nothing else but a representation of God to his people in Gospel ordinances. There they behold his glory and enjoy communion with him. He that desires communion with God in ordinances must look upon God as present: First, in majesty; second, in jealousy; third, in authority; and fourth, in purity.

Thirdly, if you would have communion with God in ordinances, then in every ordinance make communion with God your end. The hypocrisy, or the sincerity, of every man's spirit is mostly seen in his end. There's a double end that every man should propose to himself in coming to ordinances and when this end is not proposed, communion with God is not enjoyed. First, they should do them as acts of obedience in reference to God's command. Secondly, they should use them as means of communion in reference to God's promise. In every ordinance you should make communion with God your end and use the ordinance as a means for the attainment of that end. In this way, I am going to such a duty, Lord, and this is my end, to enjoy you in it. I am going to pray, and I would have the enjoyment of God in prayer. This is the end you should propound when you go about every ordinance.

Fourthly, in order to enjoy communion, get divine and spiritual apprehensions. For according to our apprehensions of God, such will be our enjoyments of him, and such will be our communions with him. Some persons have to do with God in ordinances that never think what that God is with whom they have to do. The only way to raise up our communion with God is to raise up our apprehension of him. If we know him but a little, we can never enjoy much society and communion with him.

Fifthly, in order to enjoy communion with God, make use of former experiences. The experience that men have had of the sweetness of God will stir up their hearts to long more and more after communion with God. He that has tasted of the sweetness of God cannot sit down satisfied except that he meets with God in the ordinance. *AMEN.*

FINIS.

www.ingramcontent.com/pod-product-compliance
Lightning Source LLC
Chambersburg PA
CBHW022137080426
42734CB00006B/394